L...

IS IT POSSIBLE...

Despite great efforts to address the issue of teen pregnancy, the statistics remain alarming. Two thousand unwed teenage girls in the United States will find out they are pregnant today—and that blows my mind. Gwen Diaz does an incredible job of sharing the startling statistics and substantiating them with true-life stories. In her book *Is It Possible . . . To Transform the Lives and Legacies of Single Teen Moms?* Gwen provides us with practical methods and positive solutions. She challenges us to take a new course of action and follow the examples of three women who are impacting an entire community through their ministry to teen moms. This is a challenge we can't afford to ignore.

—Dr. Tony Evans, founder and president of
The Urban Alternative; senior pastor of
Oak Cliff Bible Fellowship

Most churches hurt deeply for the people around them and genuinely want to step into their lives with substantive help and hope, but they often simply don't know what to do. Case in point: what do you do with a teenage girl who finds herself pregnant and then a young mom—especially one who has no extended family structure prepared to walk her through this radical life adjustment? In her timely book, *Is It Possible...*, Gwen Diaz uses real-life stories to help churches move from having good intentions to actually becoming Jesus' hands and heart to these fragile and often desperate young women.

—Dr. Tim Kimmel, author of *Grace-Based Parenting*
and *Grace-Filled Marriage*

Two thousand teenage girls face an unexpected pregnancy each day. Statistics like that can seem irrelevant or distant until you hear the stories behind them. Every number represents a girl in need of something only our Savior can give. So how do we, and how does the church, reach out and offer it? How can we embrace sinners without condoning sin? This book is a touching but equally practical tool that will equip, motivate, and empower you to get involved in something life-changing. If you are pro-life, this is a must read.

—Lauren Beccue, speaker and certified
sex ed instructor; author of *UN-Expecting*

IS IT POSSIBLE...

IS IT POSSIBLE...

To Transform the Lives
and Legacies of
Single Teen Moms?

YES, IT IS...

and Here's How!

By Gwendolyn
Mitchell Diaz

Deep River
B O O K S
Sisters, Oregon

IS IT POSSIBLE... To Transform the Lives and Legacies of Single Teen Moms? YES, IT IS...and Here's How!

Scripture quotations are taken from the *Holy Bible. New Living Translation* copyright© 1996, 2004, 2007 by Tyndale House Foundation, Carol Stream, Illinois 60188. All rights reserved.
When noted NIV, Scripture quotations are taken from the *Holy Bible, New International Version®, NIV®* Copyright © 1973, 1978, 1984, 2011 by Biblica, Inc.®.

Written permission to quote the lyrics from Family Tree by Matthew West granted by Matthew West personally.

Published by Deep River Books
Sisters, Oregon
http://www.deepriverbooks.com

ISBN 13: 9781940269245
ISBN 10: 1940269245
Library of Congress Control Number: 2014945921

Printed in the USA

Cover and Interior design: Juanita Dix • www.designjd.net

ACKNOWLEDGMENTS

This book could not have been written without the tremendous encouragement and support of Brad and Sue Bryant. They were instrumental in introducing me to the needs of teen moms, insistent on my participation in this book project, and actively involved throughout the entire process. Their love is not only transforming the lives and legacies of individual teenage moms (and dads), it is impacting the churches these teens attend and the communities they live in as well. My prayer is that this book will greatly multiply their amazing ministry.

TABLE OF CONTENTS

INTRODUCTION

The statistics are alarming. More than two thousand teenage girls in the United States will discover they are pregnant *today!*[1] Fourteen percent of these pregnancies will end in miscarriage. Almost one-third will be terminated by abortion.[2] Only one percent will lead to adoption.[3] That means that over half will choose to raise the child they birth, and statistically, twenty-four percent of these girls will be pregnant again before they turn twenty years old.[4] A vicious cycle is set in motion that often leads the children of these teenage moms to become teenage parents themselves.

Many organizations have realized the gravity of this situation. They have struggled to address the myriad of issues that perpetuate the cycle. The business community has created mentoring programs, workplace initiatives, and job programs designed to help young people in lower socio-economic communities discover options for their future. The health community has opened clinics (some housed in public schools) where teenage girls can confidentially seek help and alternatives to pregnancy. The educational system has reevaluated its programs and designed sex education courses for younger and younger students. Churches and other religious organizations have stepped up efforts to promote chastity and engage youth in dialogue and activities that will reinforce biblical standards and prevent pregnancy outside of marriage.

Despite all the efforts to address this issue, the cycle continues—and thousands of teenagers are left to adjust to a new identity. No longer are they simply daughters or sisters, or friends or classmates—they are moms! As their responsibilities and relationships change, they find themselves overwhelmed, exhausted, and lonely. At a time when they are most vulnerable, few churches are equipped to meet their needs. No longer do they fit in a traditional youth program, they feel out of place in a young adult class, and they cannot relate to the singles' scene. They end up dropping out.

Over the course of several weeks, I decided to randomly survey one hundred churches to see how they are dealing with this issue. They were selected from a website listing "mega churches" in the United States and Canada. A mega church by definition is a church with "a sustained average weekly attendance of 2,000 persons or more in its worship services."[5] These churches were from a variety of denominations and were located all across the United States: from Alaska to Florida; from California to New Jersey; from New Hampshire to Arizona. Their congregations were ethnically and economically diverse. Given the size of the churches and the variety of programs offered on their websites, I was certain that a majority of them would already have some kind of program in place to meet the needs of teen moms.

I found only one! So, I decided to contact the churches directly via email. Each time, I simply typed the following statement, "I was wondering if you have any special programs or resources available for teen moms."

To say I was disappointed and discouraged by the response I received is an understatement. Of the one hundred churches I contacted, only forty-six replied. Only two of them had addressed the issue at all. One had implemented a once-a-month program for teen moms and the other offered separate programs for both teen moms and teen dads that each met twice a month.

Most responses extended invitations to their youth programs. Several referred me to nearby crisis pregnancy centers. A few offered phone numbers for help lines. I was directed to agencies that housed clothing closets, offered a chance to look through a Care Closet to see if there were any baby items, and was encouraged to take a counseling course on decision-making. One church actually informed me that their receptionist had received my email but was too busy to respond due to the volume of contacts!

I am convinced that we are missing a tremendous opportunity to join God in transforming lives and impacting legacies. In order to do this, we must be willing to change. We need to examine the needs of teen moms, reevaluate the programs we currently offer, and reach out to them the same way that Christ would if he were here. We cannot continue to discard them. In 1 Corinthians 12:22-25, Paul tells us:

> Those parts of the body that seem to be weaker are indispensable, and the parts that we think are less honorable we treat with special honor. And the parts that are unpresentable are treated with special modesty, while our present-able parts need no special treatment. But God has put the body together, giving greater honor to the parts that lacked it, so that there should be no division in the body, but that its parts should have equal concern for each other (NIV).

I am not advocating in any way that we alter or remove programs that promote chastity. These are vital in the process of raising godly young men and women. And they can be very effective. What I am saying is that we need to open our eyes and extend our arms to a growing number of teen girls who so desperately need to experience Christ's love and forgiveness.

The true stories in this book will lead you from a place of despair to one of hope as you follow the lives of several teenage girls who found themselves in desperate places. You will be challenged by the commitment of three women who chose to love them and provide a place of refuge for them. You will be inspired by a church that opened its arms and a community that came to their assistance.

You will witness God's power to change hearts and lives. It is my prayer that more Christian organizations and churches will recognize the need and choose to invest in programs that really *can* transform the lives and legacies of single teen moms!

Chapter 1

IS IT POSSIBLE . . .
To Alter the Endings of Stories Like This?

September 22, 2012
Lakeland, Florida

Mallory's[6] mom had no idea what she would find when she decided to throw a load of laundry in the washing machine that hot Saturday morning. She shook her head with frustration. How many times had she asked Mallory to put her dirty clothes *in* the hamper instead of dropping them on the floor in the back of her closet? As she sorted through disheveled clothing and mismatched shoes, she found herself holding her breath. The softball uniform and socks must have been there a long time, because they were certainly starting to stink.

As she picked up the last of the smelly clothes in her fourteen-year-old's closet, Vanessa Grayson discovered a box that was damp and disintegrating. Obviously *this* was the source of the odor. What had Mallory been up to now?

Certainly she wouldn't have purposely hidden a dead rat in there, would she? But that's what it smelled like.

Vanessa lifted the lid, keeping the box as far from her nose as her arms would allow. The stench made her eyes water. She blinked to clear them as she picked out what appeared to be a pair of blood-stained underwear. Could these possibly be Mallory's? Next to them was a pair of pajama shorts she knew belonged to her daughter. And then there was a bloody towel with something wrapped up inside.

Vanessa unwrapped it carefully, trying not to allow the contents to fall onto the carpeted floor. There it was— the source of the horrific odor! And sure enough, it was a dead animal of some sort! "Mallory!" she yelled.

Wait . . . what was it?

No! This couldn't possibly be true! She closed her eyes tightly, then opened them again, hoping the image had changed. But it hadn't. It was all too clear! It was—a baby! A human baby! A fully-developed baby boy!

How could a baby have ended up in a clump of dirty laundry in the bottom of Mallory's closet? What kind of cruel trick was this? It didn't dawn on her that the baby could possibly be her own grandchild—that Mallory had given birth without letting her know she was even pregnant. No! This baby had to belong to one of Mallory's friends. Mallory must be covering for her.

Vanessa stifled a scream and ran. She found herself in the kitchen, so she dumped the contents of the box into the sink. She had to steady herself as she grabbed the phone. Was this an emergency? Should she dial 911 or should she use the non-emergency number for the police department?

Her head wasn't working right. She couldn't think things through. She couldn't make sense of anything. So she dialed her sister Phyllis and blurted out a series of incoherent phrases. All of them seemed to include the word "baby." They were punctuated by screams from Angela, Mallory's older sister, who had just walked into the kitchen.

Phyllis dropped the phone and headed straight to her sister's house. She burst into the kitchen and took one look at the nine-and-a half-pound baby cradled in the metal sink. There was no sorting it all out. There was too much hysteria. She dialed 911.

It wasn't long before the sheriff's deputies arrived. Their questions were eerily calm and routine in the midst of the chaos, and Mallory, who had appeared from somewhere in the house, was strangely composed.

What happened the morning of September 16th?

Whose baby was this in the sink?

How did it get in a box in the closet?

Mallory answered and pointed and stared unemotionally as confusion swirled around her. She described a possible miscarriage. But the questions kept coming and everything began shutting down. The mosaic of emotions inside and the bedlam of disbelief outside were too much for the fourteen-year-old to handle.

Records from September 19th revealed that the medical staff at Lakeland Regional Medical Center had contacted the police department and DCF to report the treatment and release of a Mallory Grayson for what appeared to be a miscarriage—or could it possibly have been a brutal rape? There was lots of blood.

It took several days for the truth to fully come out. But when it finally did, all the spinning thoughts that Vanessa had managed to control for so many days came crashing to the floor. They shattered into thousands of tiny pieces—propelling jagged shards that pierced deeply into everyone close to the family, severing just about every relationship that had been intact.

Mallory had been pregnant, and she had realized it. Too frightened and confused to tell anyone, she had kept it a secret. *How could she tell her family? Everything would change. She didn't want to mess things up with her Mom.*

So Mallory, a tiny, five-foot-three, 100-pound freshman in high school, had covered up the tell-tale signs by wearing baggy clothes. Some family members had suspected. After all, wasn't that boy always hanging around with his hands all over her? And why else would Mallory wear thick sweatshirts in the middle of a hot summer? Back in June, a mother from an opposing softball team had even mentioned to tournament officials that Mallory was obviously pregnant and probably should not be playing.

But Vanessa had stood up for her daughter when Mallory insisted she was not pregnant. Just to be sure, she had brought home two—not one, but two—home pregnancy tests. Yes, Vanessa had allowed her to take them privately behind the closed bathroom door, but she had trusted Mallory. She would never lie to her about this!

Both tests were negative. *Hmmph! Those nosey neighbors and relatives needed to mind their own business and find someone else to target with their suspicions and verbal assaults.*

But now, the penetrating I-told-you-so glances were destroying everything that was left of the family's self-esteem.

Mallory told the detectives that she started to feel sick on Monday and the discomfort continued until Wednesday morning. Sometime between 7 and 10 AM that morning, she had locked herself in her mother's bathroom as she went into labor. She stuffed a towel in her mouth and turned on the bathtub water to hide the noises her body was forcing her to make. As the pain grew more severe, she grabbed a pair of scissors and started to "pry the baby out." A baby boy, twenty inches long and weighing nine and a half pounds was delivered into the toilet.

Mallory felt for a pulse. The baby was alive. He moved. By then, her instincts were completely disheveled. With the umbilical cord still uniting them, she placed her hands around her baby's neck and squeezed until he stopped breathing.

She washed the baby in the sink, cleaned up the bathroom as best she could, and took a shower. Not knowing what else to do, she wrapped the body in the dirty towels and clothes and stuffed the post-partum mess in a box in the bottom of her closet.

Five days after they removed the dead baby in a box from the mobile home on a quiet tree-lined street, the detectives returned to remove a fourteen-year-old girl in handcuffs. Neither would ever return!

Mallory is being held for homicide. She is charged with first-degree murder and aggravated child abuse.

But is it possible that this story could have had a different ending?

- Is it possible . . . it could have resulted in the birth of a healthy baby boy and the healing of a hurting teenager?
- Is it possible . . . instead of feeling frightened and alone, Mallory could have discovered hope in a program designed for teen moms?
- Is it possible . . . that, while attending that program, Mallory could have been introduced to the unconditional love of Jesus Christ?
- Is it possible . . . that we can somehow transform the lives and legacies of the thousands of other struggling teens embarking on motherhood?

Chapter 2
———————

IS IT POSSIBLE . . .
For Us to Grasp the Statistics?

Mallory's story is tragic evidence of a large septic wound that is festering just below the surface of our sophisticated society. Three out of ten girls in the United States will become pregnant at least once before they are twenty years old.[7]

As was stated in the introduction, more than 2,000 teen girls in the United States will discover they are pregnant *today!* This means that close to 750,000 teens this year will struggle with some of the same emotions that eventually overwhelmed Mallory. Only one percent of these pregnant teens will choose an alternative parenting plan.[8] And statisticians have determined that up to thirty-two percent of these pregnancies will end in abortion.[9]

Despite the fact that the numbers have dropped over the past two decades, eerily synchronizing with the availability of the "morning after" pill, the teen birth rate in the

United States is still far higher than in any other industrialized country in the world. Teenagers here are two-and-a-half times more likely to have babies when compared to teens in Canada, four times more likely than teens in Germany or Norway, and almost ten times more likely than those in Switzerland. Russia is the country with the next highest teen birth rate, but an American teenage girl is still almost twenty-five percent more likely to give birth than her Russian counterpart.[10] And nearly one-quarter of these teen mothers will have a second birth before turning twenty.

Until recently, a popular premise has held that birthing a baby as a teen leads to substandard educational, financial, and social outcomes for both the mother and her child. But current studies indicate that the reverse is actually true: it is because of the bleak conditions they *already* find themselves in that young girls choose to enter the world of motherhood.[11]

These studies discovered that teen girls who grow up in poverty or in single-parent households are nearly twice as likely to give birth as girls without these disadvantages. When they feel they have little chance for advancement even if they "play by the rules," teenage girls are much more likely to opt out of mainstream economic experiences. Instead of investing their efforts in their own economic progress, they choose to invest them in raising a child.

But whether it is the baby that causes the poverty or the poverty that produces the baby, teen moms usually find themselves in a desperate situation. Traversing the road through adolescence to adulthood is a tough enough journey, but having to maneuver its twists and turns with the added responsibilities of feeding, clothing, housing, and caring for a new infant makes it almost impossible. While their friends are out partying and playing, these young moms—who are only kids themselves—are stuck at home, praying for just a few hours of uninterrupted sleep. Their lives almost invariably become a series of doctor's visits, financial difficulties, domestic and scholastic responsibilities, and relationship dilemmas.

Oddly enough, almost fifty percent of these teens never took the time to contemplate how a pregnancy would affect their lives.[12] Despite the fact that having a baby is known to be one of life's most altering events, this factor did not influence their behavioral decisions. Generally, they never made a conscious decision to become pregnant. But, then again, generally they never made a conscious effort *not to*.

With the stars of shows like MTV's *Teen Mom* and *16 and Pregnant* celebrated on TV and glamorized on magazine covers, they generally have a completely unrealistic view of what motherhood involves. So, when first confronted with the reality of her own pregnancy, a teen mom can become rather excited—even eager. A cute, cuddly, cooing baby to take to the park and dress up for birthday parties seems entertaining and rewarding. But reality proves to be much harsher.

A teen mom quickly finds herself exhausted trying to fill the many new roles she is forced to play. Besides being a new mother, she is often a student, still a daughter, sometimes an employee, and, oh, by the way, she's just a teenager. Most teenage girls experience mood swings, but as teen parents they seem to experience them much more intensely. Part of this is due to the fact that they are forced to take on so much responsibility at such a young age. It's a crash course in growing up, and it can send them reeling.

One teen mom blogged it this way, "I had a hard pregnancy but I had no idea what I was in for after he was born. For a while I didn't get a good night of sleep. My relatives stopped talking to me and began looking down on me. It was hard to see my friends living their lives and going out and hanging out on a Friday night while I stayed home. During your teenage years, it's the time to have fun and discover who you are, but I had to grow up extra fast."[13]

Another said, "Having a baby changes your whole identity. You can never go back to just being a student, a kid, or a daughter because being a mother is a lifelong responsibility. It's your job to provide for your child."[14]

Teen moms are far less likely to stay in school and receive their high school diplomas. Indeed, parenthood is the leading reason why teen girls drop out of school. It's very difficult to juggle homework and a baby. Statistically, only forty percent graduate from high school. And about one-fourth of teen moms have a second child within twenty-four months of the first birth.[15] This can further delay their ability to finish school or keep a job.

Teen moms tend to remain unmarried. Ironically, what may have started as an attempt to hang on to someone who seemed to offer a sense of security and a feeling of belonging may result in a lifetime of loneliness. Eighty percent of the dads don't stick around. When things get tough, a baby isn't enough to make them stay. It is also true that, on the average, these absent fathers pay less than $800 annually for child support, often because they are too poor themselves.

Teen moms frequently encounter a lot of criticism or negativity from their own family members. Their pregnancy sometimes comes as a shock. It is almost always a disappointment. So their parents may send messages of "You've ruined your future." "Your life is over." "Nothing good is going to happen now." "That guy is no good for you." Often ultimatums are made either by the girl's own parents or by the new set of related adults on the father's side. Sometimes the teens cannot take the pressure and move out. In Mallory's case, this was not a possibility she wished to encounter, so she took the life of her baby instead.

Two-thirds of new moms find themselves living in poverty and perpetuating a cycle that will attempt to trap their children as well. Studies show that the children of impoverished teens fare worse than other children on economic, social, and cognitive assessments.[16]

- They do worse in school than children born to older parents and are fifty percent more likely to have to repeat a grade.
- They are less likely to complete high school than children with older mothers, and have lower performances on standardized tests.
- Children who live apart from their fathers are five times more likely to be poor than children who have both parents at home.
- The daughters of teen mothers are three times more likely to become teen mothers themselves.
- And their sons are twice as likely to end up in prison.[17]

You may be wondering why more teen moms don't opt for adoption. So did I; so I asked many of them. The answer I received across the board was, "It was my choices that brought this baby into the world. The least I can do is take care of him."

One girl posted on Facebook, "Getting pregnant was the price I was willing to pay to feel connected to someone for a few minutes. Parenting my child is the price I am willing to pay to feel connected to someone for eighteen years."

Most of these girls have never experienced a real relationship, and all of them long for that. They think that the possibility of finding "forever love," as they call it, by having their own child is worth all the hardships that it could involve.

A baby provides a young girl not only with a heart attachment, but with a feeling of accomplishment. Finally, she has produced something worthwhile. Finally, there is someone in her life who needs what she has to offer. Little does she know that she is perpetuating a cycle in her child's life that might lead to the same places of loneliness and despair that she has experienced.

So, where do we as Christians find ourselves in this process?

- After all, aren't we the ones who are known for our vigilant stance outside the abortion clinics and our role in convincing these pregnant teenagers to keep their babies?
- Consequently, aren't we the ones who unintentionally assist in sentencing them to a difficult life often filled with poverty and despair?
- How can we insist that teen moms birth these babies if we don't offer any help once they do?
- Is it possible to offer help without appearing to endorse the actions that lead to birth outside of marriage?
- Is there any way that we can help remedy a situation that seems so tangled and out of our control?

Chapter 3
_____

IS IT POSSIBLE . . .
That God Is Preparing Us to Provide a Solution?

Alice hung up the phone in disbelief. It couldn't be true. She couldn't possibly have heard correctly—could she? If she dared acknowledge that the information she had just received was true, her whole world would veer off course. It could very easily crash and burn.

The fact that she was 400 miles from home when the call came didn't help matters. She realized that her son had planned it that way. He was obviously counting on distance as his ally, but perhaps it was hers, too. It was distance that allowed her to analyze rather than react. It was distance that made it possible to reason that there could have been some sort of miscommunication. It was distance that made it seem more like a bad dream and less like reality. It was distance that kept her from completely falling apart. She wasn't sure what she would have done if she had been sitting next to Sammy when he made the announcement.

She just sat there for a few minutes, struggling to get her brain under control before she shared the news with her husband. Clint had already grasped that something was very wrong.

"Isabelle is pregnant," she finally whispered while still staring into space. The words came out so calmly that she wondered for a second if they were actually hers.

"Who is Isabelle?" Clint asked, realizing that this question would probably become the opening line from a chapter he would rather exclude from the story of his life.

"The girl that Sammy has been dating," was all that Alice had to offer. She really didn't know much more. She had never met Isabelle and she could only recall Sammy mentioning her a few times.

Sammy was now living with his biological dad. He liked the freedom that came from reporting to a less-than-hands-on father figure. The few boundaries that Alice and Clint had tried to enforce hemmed him in too tightly and cramped his style. But Sammy had always remained close to his mother—even at seventeen. He had even grown to appreciate the love and acceptance he received from his stepfather, Clint. The two had become frequent hunting partners. But he preferred to live most of his life according to his own schedule and rules.

Alice's eyes finally met Clint's and the tears started to flow. Their mini-vacation was over. Yes, there were supposed to be a few more days, but there was no way they could enjoy them now, so they packed up and headed home. The drive was long and filled with unanswered questions. And the information that greeted them when they arrived did not make things any easier.

Rochelle, Isabelle's mom, did not want her daughter to keep the baby. No, she wasn't pushing for abortion—her faith would not allow that. But she felt that there was no way a fifteen- and a seventeen-year-old could raise a baby—especially two who barely knew each other! Isabelle had three years left in high school. Her life would be a mess if she didn't get a high school diploma. There was only one solution in Rochelle's mind—Isabelle must put the baby up for adoption.

Alice couldn't accept this solution. Her son was the father, and she did not want him to sign any papers that would allow someone else to raise his baby. If Sammy and Isabelle didn't want to do it, then she and Clint would! After all, this was their grandchild.

Phone calls and meetings between the two families were intense and sometimes Rochelle grew angry. Through all of the turmoil, Alice prayed and tried to remain calm and uplifting. When the phone rang, she would lay her hand on it and ask God to give her wisdom and the right words to say before she answered. Most of the time she would just listen and reassure Rochelle that everything would be okay—that God would work things out.

Alice checked out the details and found that if Isabelle chose to keep the baby, she could still graduate from high school. There were special programs for teen moms and their babies in her hometown. Plus she and Clint would make sure that the baby was taken care of if childcare became an issue.

Although Rochelle seemed to appreciate Alice's calming counsel, one month before the baby was due, she gave Isabelle an ultimatum. "If you don't sign adoption papers right now, you have to move out."

Isabelle chose the latter option and moved in with Alice and Clint and Sammy's little sister, Katie. Sammy decided to move back home too, hoping to make things work in what was a very disheveled relationship.

Alice and Clint were grateful, but realistic. "This is not going to be a fairy tale," they warned. "It's going to be very difficult. At times it will even seem like a nightmare. But we are here to help." It was during this time that Alice really learned how to pray. She learned what it meant to take her requests to God and leave them in His hands. She learned to ask God for divine guidance in every detail of her life—and her family's—during both the good moments and the bad.

The warning that Alice and Clint had given didn't come close to encompassing the reality that Sammy and Isabelle encountered once the baby was born. The two teens were in no way prepared for the difficulties they would face. Not only was there a new baby to care for once they walked into their home after a hard day at school, there were also new identities to adjust to when they walked out. They didn't seem to fit in anywhere any more. They were parents. They were in a completely different phase of life than any of their friends. Everything at school was designed for kids who had no serious external obligations. Instead of hanging out at the ball field or wandering through the mall, after-school-hours were spent sitting in a doctor's office, or standing in the checkout line at the grocery store, or trying to feed a fussy baby.

For the same reasons, they no longer fit into the comfortable niche that had been carved out for teenagers in the youth program at their church; they couldn't relate to the "twenty-somethings" who met for karaoke contests and long dinner engagements; and they were uncomfortable hanging out with other new parents who were happily married. They suddenly found themselves in a position that no one else seemed to understand or accept.

The young couple withdrew from everything that had been meaningful in their lives and began to look to each other for comfort and camaraderie. But they were too young and too exhausted to handle the pressure, and it wasn't long before their relationship began to implode. It took about a year for the stress and turmoil to reach a level that neither could tolerate, and eventually Sammy moved out.

For another year, Alice and Clint lovingly ministered to the mom who had birthed their grandson, teaching her about God's love and demonstrating it in tangible ways. Due to the sacrificial love they demonstrated every day,

Isabelle was finally able to understand and accept the sacrifice that Jesus had made for her on the cross. She invited Him into her life—not only to redeem her soul, but also to repair the damage that had taken place in her life. She felt it was time for her to return home and allow Jesus to heal the relationships that had been shattered within her own family. She took the baby with her.

For almost three tumultuous, chaotic years, Alice and Clint had poured themselves out in an effort to make things work for Isabelle and Sammy and their new grandson. When Isabelle chose to leave, Alice began to wonder: *What else could we have done? Why did nobody step in to help us? If this is so difficult for two teens who were raised in good homes, how much worse must it be for others who come from homes that don't include love as a foundation? What happens to those girls—and their babies? Is there anywhere they can go for help?* These questions disturbed her. Searching her mind for answers often kept her awake at night.

Meanwhile, Alice and Clint began attending a new church. Clint fit right in, helping with the Awana program for kids just as he had in their previous church. Katie loved her new youth group. Several of her good friends from school already attended. Sammy even showed up on occasion and actually enjoyed the services. But Alice felt like a stranger. She had no idea where she could fit in. At her previous church, she had always been the one to organize women's ministries events and host any and every occasion that benefited from food or hospitality.

When her husband encouraged her to just jump in somewhere and get involved at their new church, she replied, "God hasn't told me what to do yet." So she continued to attend services while she prayed and waited.

Several months later, one of the leaders from the MOPS (Mothers of Pre-Schoolers) Program approached Alice and explained that she and several other women had been praying about starting a Teen MOPS program. They had sensed a great need in their town and were trying to put a team together to help on Wednesday evenings. She still needed someone to help with hospitality—to make sure there were centerpieces on the tables and food for the girls to munch on. She had heard that Alice was very good at that sort of thing. And, oh and by the way, was it true that she had personal experience in mentoring a teenage mom, because that could really come in handy?

Alice did not jump at the opportunity. As a matter of fact, she wanted to run in the opposite direction. There was no way she wanted to invest any more of herself in that department of life. Certainly this couldn't be what God had in mind for her. He knew how tough it had been— and, for that matter, still was. The pain was far too close to the surface to head in that direction again.

Later that week at the dinner table, she shared with her husband and daughter that the MOPS leader at the church had asked her to become involved in the new teen program. Katie spoke up, "Mom, don't you think that's what God has been preparing you for?"

Alice didn't reply. She couldn't. She knew that her daughter was right, but she didn't want to admit it.

The next week she found herself setting up the tables and arranging the snacks she had picked up on the way to the Teen MOPS program. When she was finished, she sat in the back of the room, waiting for the meeting to be over so she could clean up and complete her new duties. A few of the girls walked over to thank her for the food. Over the next few weeks, she got to know their names and a little bit about their lives. As more girls attended, Alice realized it would be helpful if she sat at one of the tables to help maintain order.

Soon Alice was filling the role of a mentor as well as handling all of the hospitality. The girls recognized that she was someone who truly understood what they were going through. She understood the loneliness and exhaustion that accompanied being a teen mom. She understood the frustrations of trying to maintain family relationships. She understood that they needed honest words to direct them and loving arms to embrace them. She understood that what they needed most was God's grace to rescue and sustain them. She became a counselor and a confidant and a best friend. "Alice is the mother we all wish we had," one of the girls recently affirmed.

So when the coordinator of the Teen MOPS program decided it was time to move on to another area of ministry, Alice was the obvious choice to take her place. Once again, she hesitated, but it didn't take long for her, with the help of Clint and Katie, to realize that, although it might not be part of her plan, this was the next logical step in God's agenda for her life.

Everything she had been through with Sammy and Isabelle had been difficult, so difficult that there were still places in her heart that ached very deeply. But she realized that God could use her pain to help others heal. He had uniquely prepared her to touch the lives of these girls. So she threw herself in wholeheartedly.

God's plan took her far outside the boundaries of her own comfort zone and assigned her to a place that required total dependence on Him. "But how many people in the Bible actually got to work within their comfort zones?" she asks. "I can't think of any. Why should I expect that God would let me?"

His plan taught her to pray. It forced her to trust Him. "There's no way I could be doing this if God had not prepared me," she now explains as she stands up in front of dozens of girls who are looking to her for leadership. "God wants to do amazing things through your experiences, too, if you will let Him," she adds. But there were times when Alice felt completely overwhelmed!

Chapter 4

_____

IS IT POSSIBLE . . .
That God Is Preparing Others to Work Beside Us?

By her own definition, Carolyn was a "hot mess" during her teen years. She grew up on the streets and did whatever it took to survive. When her own brother threatened to shoot her, she escaped to Miami to live with an aunt who worshiped and worked in a church near her home. Just about every day, Carolyn walked through those church doors with her aunt accompanying her as she cleaned and cooked and attended services. She learned a lot about what it means to be Christian and, for a while, she tried to pull it off. But when she showed up drunk at a church New Year's Eve Party, she—and everyone around her—realized that she was living a lie.

Carolyn moved in with the parents of a guy she was dating. She had already completed her GED and was working three part-time jobs in order to survive. But one day she discovered that her boyfriend was cheating on her. She left and stayed wherever she could find a place to lie down, until a family from her aunt's church finally took her in. When she was ready, they even helped her rent her own apartment and get on her feet.

She was in the middle of this very tumultuous time when she met Dwight. She had been dating one of his friends until one night when that friend's anger became physical. Carolyn confided in Dwight and found a friend she could trust. She never intended to fall in love, but somehow Dwight knew that this was the girl God wanted him to marry. His low-key, loving care helped her realize that she needed him and his godly influence in her life. Every time they hit a snag in their relationship, he was willing to wait and pray for her. When she finally gave her heart completely to Christ, it was with Dwight.

They attended church together regularly, and it wasn't very long until they found themselves walking down the aisle. Five months later, at the age of twenty, Carolyn was pregnant with their first child. Not having much money, they prayed for God to show them how and where they could best serve Him.

While visiting some friends in central Florida, Dwight drove Carolyn past her grandmother's old house. "I sure wish we could live there," she sighed nostalgically. But with a three-month-old, no visible job opportunity, and no other real ties to the area, it was little more than the verbalization of a childhood fantasy.

However, when Dwight received a job offer at a ministry in central Florida, Carolyn realized that it was God who had stirred the longing. With God's leading and the help of a government grant, they were able to move into the house she adored. How could they ever doubt God's goodness!

They easily found a new church home at First Baptist Church at the Mall. While Carolyn attended services, she kept her eyes and ears open for an opportunity to serve. She was very interested in joining the drama team, but rehearsal times did not work out. Meanwhile, she began to attend the Tuesday morning MOPS group. It wasn't long before she was asked to help with the Teen MOPS program that was just getting off the ground. "No way!" was her initial response. "That is not where I belong."

Although she had experienced just about every aspect of teen street life, Carolyn had never been a teen mom. She didn't feel that there was any way she could relate to the girls in the program. But Alice, who had just been asked to direct the program, kept asking her and insisting that she give it a try. She finally gave in.

Carolyn was given the task of soliciting donations to stock the MOPS shop. So every week she spent hours phoning and emailing companies and individuals, trying to convince them to donate car seats, baby carriers, bottles, cribs, diapers, and anything else a young mom could need. In addition, she attended and helped at all the weekly meetings.

She was equipped with a perspective that Alice could not provide. When excess compassion caused Alice to become indulgent with the girls, or her emotions threatened to skew the boundaries that had carefully been established, Carolyn's realistic outlook came into play. "You need diapers already? Why? What happened? What went wrong that you ran out so soon?" she would ask rather than just hand out another package. "You've got to plan better than that."

Carolyn had grown up experiencing the consequences of parental irresponsibility. She had lived through cold days without power and long nights with no adequate roof over her head. She was determined not to allow these girls to impose that lifestyle on their children. She knew what it took to graduate from high school when no one else gave her a fighting chance. She knew how important it was to make good choices despite the effort and energy needed to follow through.

Carolyn knew that these girls God had assigned to her could and should challenge the lifestyle they had grown up in, because she had—and she had won! "I know you can do it better. I know you can do it right," she confronted them. "I know, because I did it."

While God was using the streets of Miami to prepare Carolyn for ministry, He was also equipping someone else in a very different way.

• • •

Debbie loved babies. She always had. So when she and Blake got married, they knew it wouldn't be long before they would start their very own family. She eagerly anticipated the day she would be snuggling a newborn baby in her arms. But month after month passed by, leaving disappointment in its wake. Those long, suspenseful months turned into extremely long, discouraging years, and the routine of anticipation followed by disappointment became almost unbearable. The doctors insisted that there was no medical reason for them not to have children. All the money Blake made as a professional golfer wasn't able to fix the problem. They were encouraged to "just keep trying." So they did.

Meanwhile it was hard to attend baby showers— especially if the new parents joked about the fact that they "weren't even trying" while Debbie and Blake were trying so hard! All the other young couples they had hung out with when they were first married were now raising families, and they were left alone to figure out new ways to entertain themselves. Life just wasn't turning out the way it was supposed to.

Instead of finding herself angry with others, Debbie developed a growing disappointment in herself that spilled over into her relationship with God. Thoughts of getting pregnant initially consumed her, but discouraging thoughts of never getting pregnant took their place. Lack of fertility and years of frustration ultimately led to feelings of failure.

Blake and Debbie realized it was time to seek an alternative. After nine long years of disappointment, they came to the realization that adoption was the only choice they had if they ever wanted a family of their own. So they began the long process of filling out papers, answering questions, and feeling like their lives were being put on trial and cross-examined. But God's fingerprints were all over the adoption process. There was convincing evidence of His divine involvement.

February 14, 1991 became a Valentine's Day they will never forget as they packed and prepared for a long trip to Rapid City, South Dakota to meet a three-week-old baby boy who would forever share their name. On February 16, little Matthew was welcomed into their lives, bringing with him all the hope and joy a child can possibly bring.

A year and a half later, much to everyone's shock and delight, Debbie discovered she was pregnant. Oh the ecstasy! Oh the fear! *Could she possibly love this child as much as the one God had already placed in her arms?* Those nine months both flew and crept by in one emotional blur, and on April 26, 1993, Luke joined his two-year-old, big brother.

When friends commented on the miracle that had taken place, referring to the fact that she had been able to conceive and birth a child, Debbie silently shook her head. She knew that the real miracle was not the fact that she had finally become pregnant, but the fact that she had NOT become pregnant during all those previous years.

No doctor had ever found a reason for her infertility. But now she knew why: if God had allowed her to become pregnant any of the times she had pleaded with Him to open her womb, Matthew would never have become a part of their family.

The struggle and heartaches of infertility gave Debbie a deep, personal insight into the value of life. She couldn't understand why so many babies were being aborted when there were so many homes longing to embrace them. She began to attend pro-life rallies and functions. It didn't seem fair that all some girls had to do was lie down with a guy and they seemed to get pregnant, while others struggled through every medical procedure available only to be let down over and over again. It made her angry that some women so flippantly chose to discard a life that came about too easily, while the others spent so much of their time and efforts and finances trying to produce a life that never developed. It seemed so unjust. Debbie wasn't only pro-life; she was very pro-adoption. She understood very clearly from her own experience how, when handled correctly, the process can benefit everyone:

- Although it requires great sacrifice, the birth mom can be released from a difficult situation that might otherwise cause great duress. Financial difficulties are no longer compounded and relational issues are often relieved. She can have a sense of peace and satisfaction in knowing that someone else will love and care for her baby in a way that she is unable to offer. Teen moms are given the opportunity to complete their education and grow up without the demands of parenthood.

- Babies can benefit from the love and support of parents who have the emotional resources to embrace them and the financial ability to care for them.
- The adoptive family can experience the joy and blessing of adding a new life to their family—often fulfilling an otherwise illusive dream.

Debbie passionately spoke of her feelings to Blake. When he suggested that she capitalize on her pro-life, pro-adoption stance by volunteering at the local Crisis Pregnancy Center, Debbie was hesitant. She was very private about her feelings, and somewhat insecure about her ability to contribute. But he insisted—knowing that she had so much to offer. Finally she agreed to step outside of her comfort zone and give it a try.

From the very beginning she was hooked. Not only was her life being changed in the process, so were the lives of many young teens—and their babies! The difficulties she had been through gave her the credibility and experience she needed to make an impact. Often she was able to dissuade young girls from having an abortion by sharing her own story of adoption. Sometimes, the fact that Debbie was willing to hold a young girl's hand through an ultrasound procedure caused that girl to fall in love with the life that was stirring inside her womb.

One time, a young teen, who was adamant about having an abortion, came through the clinic doors. Debbie interviewed her and skillfully wove the possibility of keeping the child and allowing it to be brought up in a loving home into the conversation. She asked the girl to consider returning for an ultrasound procedure before she made her final decision.

When the pregnant teen left, Debbie pleaded with God to help her change her mind. The girl returned for the ultrasound as well as a few more visits. Then suddenly she stopped coming to her appointments. The only telephone number Debbie had for her was disconnected. She feared the worst. She was sure the girl had gone ahead with her plans to have an abortion.

A few months later, Debbie was in Hawaii on a business trip with her husband when she received an early morning phone call. Although it was only six o'clock in Hawaii, it was noon in Florida when the receptionist at the clinic dialed Debbie to inform her that the girl they had been praying for had just dropped off an envelope with Debbie's name on the outside. Holding her breath, Debbie instructed the receptionist to open it. It was an invitation to a baby shower! Debbie was ecstatic. To say it made her day is a huge understatement. It made her life—and all the pain that she had experienced in the process of creating her own family—worthwhile.

When another young teen was incredibly torn between the demands of an angry mother who insisted she have an abortion, and the desires of her own heart to keep her baby, Debbie realized that she needed to find a way to expose "her girls" to more consistent mentoring and support. Seeing them for once-a-month, follow-up appointments didn't afford enough time to make any real difference in their lives. When she discovered a brochure for a new Teen MOPS program that had been left at the clinic, she realized that this was the venue she had been praying for.

At first, it was her goal just to introduce girls to the program and hope they would choose to get involved. But soon she realized that the young teens she was dealing with required transportation in order to attend. So she agreed to pick them up and take them to the meetings and then deliver them back home. Occasionally she would check on them during the meetings, and soon she found herself sitting at one of the tables in order to help keep order and lead discussions. Teen MOPS offered her a way to follow-up with the girls she was seeing for brief visits at the clinic. It provided one-on-one time for conversations and in-depth time to teach and mentor.

Alice and Carolyn recognized a kindred spirit in Debbie, and it wasn't long before all three of them were working together. Alice provided much of the food and hospitality for the meetings, and picked up many of the girls on her way to the church. She set the agenda and led the meetings. Carolyn continued to solicit donations, organize the Bible studies, and pray a lot. Since Debbie didn't have a full time job, she was able to stay in touch with the girls during the week. She assisted with transportation to Teen MOPS, provided items needed during the meetings, and operated a shop where the girls could "purchase" donated items they needed for themselves and their babies.

All three leaders focused on sharing truths from the Bible and teaching the girls how to apply them to their life situations. They brought in guest speakers who offered tips on everything from bathing new babies, to filling out resumes for after-school jobs.

They made a dynamic team. When either Alice's or Debbie's kindness clouded their vision, Carolyn challenged them. When Carolyn's realism hampered her ministry, Alice or Debbie reminded her of Christ's unconditional love. Despite their completely different backgrounds and personalities and life experiences, God was able to forge three disparate women into a dynamic team—a team that became vigorously committed to loving teen moms enough to transform their lives and change their legacies. In the next chapter we will take a look at the program they developed for teen moms.

A letter from Blake to Matthew's birth mom prior to his adoption:

Dear Birthmother,

A few weeks ago, very early in the morning, my wife got out of bed to use the restroom. She came back to bed in tears because her period had arrived and she was once again very disappointed not to be pregnant. I can only imagine your tears when you found out you were pregnant and the hurt you have gone through to arrive at the point of placing your child for adoption. It is my firm belief, however, that all the tears can become tears of joy as together we bring an individual to full adulthood; happy, joyful, well-adjusted, and well-loved. . .

. . . I realize the decision you have made is difficult, maybe the hardest thing you have ever done. Giving birth to your child and allowing someone else to raise it must be very scary. I will not pretend to understand what you must be going through. Please know that your child is a blessing to this world and will be the greatest of blessings to us or some other adoptive parents. I feel strongly about children knowing they are loved and wanted and in a secure place. Your child will know of his adoption as well as your love. Your child will understand the sacrifice you have made and will be taught to love you in return.

Sometimes out of great pain comes great healing and lasting joy. It is my wish and prayer that our child, longed for by us, and agonized over by you, will be happy and we will all know God's peace.

God bless you,
The prospective adoptive father

A letter from Debbie to Matthew's birth mom thirteen years after his adoption:

July 26, 2004

Dear J*,

I don't know if you will ever read this letter but I feel a strong calling from God to write it. I just want to say thank you so much for choosing life almost fourteen years ago when you found out you were pregnant. Thank you too for loving the baby you bore so much that you wanted a better life for him. Thank you for allowing us to raise him as our son. He is thirteen now and is becoming a young man. It seems those toddler days were just a blink away, and I know that in another blink or two he will be an adult on his own.

I just want you to know that I think of you often and am so grateful for the sacrifices you made to bring him into this world and to bring him into our family.

I have especially had you on my heart the past month. I have been asked to be a counselor at a crisis pregnancy center and I have been feeling woefully unequipped to do that. But every time I think of a reason why I shouldn't, I think of you and I think of our son. Someone must have "been there" for you fourteen years ago to give you wisdom, guidance, and hope. And out of my gratitude to you, I feel it is now my turn to do the same for someone else.

Thank you again. I pray that your life has been blessed.

In His love,

Debbie

Chapter 5
_____

IS IT POSSIBLE . . .
To Create a Program Just for Teen Moms?

None of the churches Alice had attended over the years met the needs of teen parents. This was particularly evident in the case of her son and the mother of her grandbaby. No matter where they went, they always felt uncomfortable—sometimes even unwanted. Everyone tried to fit them into existing church programs rather than reach out to them in their own unique circumstances or take into account their own distinct hardships.

Alice was familiar with the story told by the apostle Paul in the sixth chapter of Acts. She realized that sometimes even the apostles had to get creative and initiate new programs in order to meet the needs of disenfranchised people. She wanted to create a space where the overlooked young "widows" she was called to serve could feel worthwhile; a place where they could be cherished and cared for; a place where their lives could be transformed by the love of Jesus and the power of the Holy Spirit; a place where they could be fed.

So, starting with just a few teenage girls, their babies, the blessings of the church staff, and a lot of prayer, Alice began to lead the Teen MOPS program in her church in a new direction. From the very beginning she realized she had to think outside the box. She knew she had to venture outside the safe, comfortable walls of the church and be willing to step inside the girls' neighborhoods and homes.

None of the girls who were interested in attending the new program could drive, so Alice arranged to pick them up. This allowed her to meet their family members and friends. The pick-up places weren't generally very attractive and the people weren't always very nice but, faithfully, week after week, she began to earn their trust.

Alice always insisted on meeting each girl's parents and telling them where she was taking their daughter and what time they could expect her home. One night as she dropped off one of the girls, some of the neighborhood boys began to taunt Alice. The girl she had just dropped off came storming out of her house, got in their faces, and adamantly declared, "Don't ya'll be talking like that to Ms. Alice. She's a church lady!" She stared at the boys with her hands on her hips until each one of them quietly retreated from the area and Alice was able to back her car out. Although she continued to encounter the boys, Ms. Alice never experienced any more problems.

Since each of the girls came with at least one infant in tow, it was logical for Teen MOPS to meet on Wednesday evenings. The church already provided childcare for several other classes that met that night.

Alice was assigned a small meeting room with very few amenities—just some tables and chairs and a nearby restroom, but it was adequate. Soon she realized that she needed to find a way to convince the girls that it was best to drop their children off in the nursery instead of bringing them to the MOPS room. She wasn't sure if it was an issue of trust or if the girls enjoyed the attention their babies brought, but it was hard to accomplish anything meaningful with so many children requiring attention.

A system utilizing "Mommy Bucks" was put in place. The girls were rewarded with play money for completing certain tasks and activities. With this money they could "buy" items for their babies from a supply closet that Alice and new volunteer Carolyn would stock with donations. Among the tasks were:
- Bringing their Bibles,
- Finding their own transportation,
- Providing confirmation of doctor's check-ups for themselves and their babies,
- Showing a bulletin from a church service they had attended, AND . . .
- Dropping their children off in the nursery.

IT WORKED!

Every other week, they opened the "MOPS Shop" so the girls could do their "shopping." Through this process they learned to plan ahead and spend wisely so they could get the items they really needed. Before long, larger and even more important tasks were added to the activities that earned "Mommy Bucks," including choosing to nurse their baby, receiving their high school diploma, being baptized, and dedicating their child to the Lord.

The system was a winner. The girls loved earning diapers and wipes and blankets and furniture. Carolyn made it her job to acquire anything the girls needed. She spent hours calling individuals and businesses to ask for donations. Soon there were car seats and strollers and cribs and changing tables waiting for the girls.

Even though the girls had to "earn" the items they took home, they were taught to treat them as blessings. If there were no wipes one week, they learned not to be upset. Together they thanked God for the ones He had provided in the weeks before.

Since none of the girls had their own Bibles, each girl who attended was given one on her first visit. The leaders figured that even if they never came back, at least they would have their very own Bible to read when they were ready. Alice and Carolyn allotted most of the five-hundred-dollar budget they received to providing a Bible for each girl.

Although Bible study was only planned twice a month, the girls brought their Bibles every week, ready to check out any passages that might come up in their conversations. Soon they requested that Bible study time be increased to three weeks every month. Alice and Carolyn and Debbie (who had now come on board) were very happy to oblige. They studied the basic foundations of the Christian faith as well as lessons from books such as *Bad Girls in the Bible* by Liz Curtis Higgs[18] and a Bible study titled *More Beautiful You* written by Christian musician Jonny Diaz.[19] The girls were excited to discover how relevant the Bible was to their lives. They began to look for ways to apply the lessons during the week.

The weeks without Bible study offered a wide variety of interesting and fun events. Speakers from the community encouraged the girls to get their high school diplomas and showed them how they could afford a college education. They taught them how to fill out resumes and how to dress and handle themselves during job interviews. Sometimes there were crafts they could make or projects they could do to help others.

Some of the girls had never had their picture taken with their babies, so Carolyn began to chronicle the milestones in their babies' lives with her new camera. When babies were birthed, she made hospital visits to record their first few moments of life. Those pictures led to invitations to birthday parties and baby dedications and even weddings! During her solicitations, Carolyn came across a company that was willing to develop all the girls' pictures for free, and Debbie provided the materials for each girl to make her very own scrapbook. Scrapbooking became a favorite activity at the meetings.

Of course, there was food every week. Snacks gave way to healthy meals, usually home-cooked by one of the leaders. Once in a while they brought in subs or pizza, and sometimes another group from the church offered to provide the food. Any leftovers were carefully bagged up and sent home with very grateful girls.

As you might guess, the group began to grow. From three skeptical young moms, the numbers quickly grew to a dozen; then twenty; and before long, more than thirty teenage moms and their babies were attending each week.

Soon it became necessary to assign the girls to tables. A leader sat at each one to maintain order and monitor discussions. They not only mentored "their girls" during the meetings, they took it upon themselves to check on them during the week.

As much time as they spent planning and preparing each session, the leaders could be assured of two things:

1. Things would never go exactly as planned. The homes these girls came from were very chaotic and some of that chaos came with them. They quickly learned that flexibility was a vital asset in programming the meetings. One girl's crisis could result in a powerful group discussion. Another girl's joy could infect the whole group.

2. Most of the real ministry took place outside of the church's walls. Phone numbers were exchanged with

the leaders so the girls could call with any questions or problems. A private Facebook page was established so the group could stay connected during the week. When anyone had a medical emergency, they called Carolyn who (despite the fact that she had two young children of her own) rushed them to the hospital and stayed with them until family members could arrive. Debbie often opened her home to young ladies who needed a quiet retreat from their hectic lives. Alice was quick to pick up food at the church's Compassion House and deliver it to any of the girls who were desperately short. Often she would drop by their homes with extra diapers just to check on how they were doing.

The leaders began inviting the girls to worship services and provided transportation when it was needed. They sat with them through the services and answered any questions they had. They helped the girls understand what was being taught and encouraged them to incorporate it into their lives. But the most important thing they did was to pray faithfully and fervently for each of "their girls!"

Chapter 6

IS IT POSSIBLE . . .
To Help One Teen Mom Discover Hope?

If anyone had cared enough to watch her as she trudged those last few blocks home from school, they would have realized that something was bothering the twelve-year-old girl who lived at the end of the block. Her backpack was always heavy since she was good about bringing her schoolwork home, but there was something else that seemed to be weighing her down that day. Something very burdensome.

Mercedes hadn't told anyone—especially not Jason, the sixteen-year-old guy from down the street who would no doubt be showing up at her house in a little while—but she was beginning to suspect that she might be pregnant. Nothing seemed right inside her body. She constantly felt sick and was always so tired. She had never liked PE very much, but now, having to run around in the hot Florida sun felt like torture. As she climbed the few steps to the front door, she noticed that her feet and ankles had begun to swell.

She made her way through the tiny living room and into her bedroom. She meant to deposit just her backpack on the bed, but her whole body went down with it. She laid there, sprawled on her back like a rag doll for about ten minutes. Then she pulled her arms out of the straps, sat herself up, and headed to the bathroom—again. She had gone just before leaving school, but she was always having to go these days. Her teachers were getting perturbed with her multiple requests for hall passes.

She washed her hands and splashed some water on her face, hoping to somehow chase the weariness away. She glanced in the mirror. Her face was swollen, and she hadn't even been crying. She bit her lip. She knew the truth. She had been around enough friends and relatives who had gone through the same thing that she could figure it out for herself.

Apparently her mother, Loretta, knew too. Late that night, when she arrived home with her usual lover, she starting asking questions, *Why was Mercedes so droopy the last few weeks? Did she realize she was gaining weight? What was going on?* Finally, she declared, "Girl, you better not be pregnant, 'cause if you are, we aren't keeping it. It costs too much to raise a baby—and we don't have that kind of money."

A few days later, Loretta came home with a pregnancy test in her hand. She sent Mercedes into the bathroom to take it, muttering threatening remarks about any possible results.

Mercedes stared at the stick, waiting, and praying that somehow she could be wrong. She didn't have to wait long to find out. Two telltale pink lines appeared almost immediately. Her body heaved and she gulped back the tears. She tried not to think too much, but thoughts kept breaking through the barrier she was desperately trying to erect. *Guess I had it coming. I knew we shouldn't be doing it unprotected. But he was so adamant—so sure he could pull out in time. I knew better, but I didn't want to lose him. He is the only one who cares. Maybe he'll love me even more if I have his baby.*

Her mother didn't need to ask. She could tell by the distressed look on Mercedes' face when she finally opened the bathroom door. The hot words and angry gestures that followed couldn't make her feel any worse than she already did. There was no room in her brain for them, so they just kept bouncing off like they were hitting a brick wall. It wasn't that she was indifferent—she was just numb.

Her mother's reaction added another layer to the loneliness that was enveloping her, adding to the distance she already felt. *Where had her mother been when she needed her? Why was she never home? Why was going to a casino more important than being with her? Maybe if she had been here and given her some attention instead of . . .*

Over the next few days, Loretta insisted more and more vehemently that her daughter have an abortion. She gave her an ultimatum, "Either you go have the abortion I scheduled for next week or you're out of here—you're living on your own!"

So Mercedes left! At twelve years old she went to live with an older cousin who agreed that abortion was not the right choice. *After all, it was her fault that she was pregnant, not the baby's, so it shouldn't have to be the one to suffer.* Jason supported her decision, which made Mercedes even more certain that she was making the right one.

When she was about two months pregnant, another cousin offered to take her for a medical evaluation at the crisis pregnancy center nearby. She figured that, since it was free, it was the least she could do for her baby. That was where Mercedes first met Debbie, who was volunteering at *A Woman's Choice Crisis Pregnancy Center* that day.

Mercedes dutifully filled out all the forms and went through the necessary "first visit" procedures. But she was quick to point out that her biggest concern was finding out if her mother could legally force her to have an abortion— something Loretta still insisted was going to happen, but something Mercedes more stubbornly and resolutely opposed with each confrontation.

The clinic staff carefully explained that, even though she was a minor, this was Mercedes' decision to make. They showed her the legal documents proving that her mother could not legally impose her demands. Mercedes was relieved. She even smiled a little. At the end of her appointment she was asked if she would like to have an ultrasound so she could see the baby that was growing inside her. This time a big smile crossed her face, and a small nod indicated that she would, so the procedure was scheduled for the next week.

Debbie offered to accompany Mercedes through the ultrasound even though it was not her scheduled day to work at the clinic. Surprised that any adult who didn't have to was interested in helping her, Mercedes shrugged and almost inaudibly replied, "That would be OK."

Sure enough, Mercedes showed up on time, and Debbie was there to hold her hand. Mercedes' eyes grew wide as the baby's image came up on the screen. They filled with tears as she examined her baby's tiny features; and watched his heart beat; and saw his reactions to the poking and prodding of the clinician. She quietly sobbed as she realized that the tiny life inside her was a real person and no one could take it away.

Debbie exchanged phone numbers with Mercedes' cousin so that they could stay in touch, but only a few days later that contact number no longer worked. For some reason the phone had been shut off. Debbie had a home phone number for Mercedes' mom, but as much as she wanted to, she knew it was too risky to dial it. It could very easily create problems for Mercedes if her mom was not aware of her clinic visits. Plus it was very likely that she had no idea where her daughter was now staying anyway. Many times Debbie drove past the building the cousin had mentioned as her place of employment, but she never was able to spot the car that Mercedes had climbed into as she left the clinic a few days earlier.

Several weeks later, as Debbie was going through some paperwork, she mentioned to the volunteer at the desk that it was probably time to close Mercedes' file. They had not heard from her in a long time and there was no way to reach her.

"Mercedes Washington?" the assistant asked. "She's in the back right now having a Life Steps Appointment. She showed up this morning."

Debbie's jaw dropped. *Mercedes had not moved out of town. And she had not had an abortion. Her baby was still alive!* She scrambled to find the brochure she had that would introduce her to Teen MOPS. She felt that Mercedes needed a place to plug in; a place where she could feel wanted and loved; a place where she could get the attention and instruction she needed to help her care for this baby; a place where she could learn about Jesus. Teen MOPS was the perfect place.

Debbie could hardly wait for Mercedes to finish her appointment. She realized that Mercedes might not even remember her, but maybe she would at least listen to her about the program. She waited anxiously in the hallway.

This time it was Mercedes' jaw that dropped as she stepped out of the appointment room and ran smack into Ms. Debbie. "You're the one that saw my baby on the ultrasound with me," she exclaimed.

Debbie reached out and gave her a big hug. She shared how worried she had been for her and how much she had prayed. Then she handed Mercedes the brochure and explained the special program that was designed just for teen moms. She mentioned that some weeks there was a Bible study and other weeks there were guest speakers from the community, but always there was a dinner provided. In addition, she explained that the girls could earn points to "purchase" various items they needed for their babies—everything from diapers and wipes to car seats and strollers. Debbie offered to find someone to pick Mercedes up if she wanted to go, since she was going to be out of town for a few weeks.

To Debbie's amazement, Mercedes accepted the offer. *After all, who could refuse free food for themselves, and diapers and other nice things for their baby?*

"The first time I walked in to Teen MOPS I felt like everybody already knew me and loved me," she explains in her deep, soft voice. I kept going back, not just for the free food and things for my baby, but because I knew I needed the connection. I needed people I could talk to, people who would listen to me and give me advice. After four or five times it felt like where I belonged."

Kobe was born that fall to a thirteen-year-old mother. Several of the Teen MOPS leaders were in the hospital with her the whole time she was in labor. They knew that even with all the strength that it took to stand up against her mother's demands to abort her baby, Mercedes was still only thirteen years old—a little girl struggling with little girl needs. She needed all the care and help they could offer.

Life didn't suddenly get a whole lot better for Mercedes. The teenager still bounced around from one cousin's house to another's, and for a short time she lived with her grandmother, but through all the external confusion, Teen MOPS provided a place of acceptance and stability. It offered encouragement and support. It gave her a framework for making wise decisions.

Mercedes gave her life to Christ at a special outreach sponsored by the church that fall and a few weeks later she chose to be baptized. "I knew it was the right time. It was the next step. It was obedience and a way of showing my faith was real." Soon she joined the church, and she continues to attend regularly. One of her first steps after becoming a member was to publicly dedicate her baby to the Lord. She loves her new church and all that it means to her. "I miss it a lot if I can't go. I really feel like I belong."

When I interviewed Mercedes, I sat down to talk to a soft-spoken, mature young lady, who is now sixteen years old. She seemed much wiser than her years should allow. Jason is no longer a part of her life. The choices and decisions he is making no longer fit with the priorities she has set for herself and her baby. She recently moved back in with her mother. Her grandmother paved the way for reconciliation by reminding Loretta, "I didn't kick you out when you were a teen mom. I let you keep your babies." Loretta helps Mercedes care for Kobe and "spoils him rotten." And she now welcomes visits from Ms. Debbie and the other leaders from Teen MOPS.

Mercedes has only one year left before her high school graduation. She will not only graduate with a diploma, but will also have two certificates—one that will allow her to get a job immediately as an EKG technician and the other as a CNA. But her plans don't stop there. She wants to become an RN.

Mercedes is realistic about her present as well as her future. She admits there are days that it isn't fun being a mother and a full-time student. Some days are filled with parenting frustrations, long hours of study, and trips to the ER. But she wouldn't be willing to trade the journey God is taking her on for anything. She glances over at a happy three-year-old pushing a big, blue truck and smiles, "Teen MOPS has helped me a lot! It gave me hope. It changed my life! I tell everybody I know, 'cause I want their lives to change, too."

Chapter 7

IS IT POSSIBLE . . .
For that Teen's Hope to Become Contagious?

Mercedes was able to keep up with her schoolwork by attending the Teen Parent program offered at Traviss Career Center. She told new classmates there all about Teen MOPS and she invited them to join her. Many of them did, and the program experienced a sudden growth. "No doubt, the free food makes them want to come," she giggles, adding, "We have a lot of greedy girls. But once they get there, they like the whole program."

Anna was one of Mercedes new friends who started attending. She too found hope and life in Jesus Christ. And the feelings of value and affirmation she experienced at Teen MOPS allowed her to reach out to a very lonely, very desperate friend who showed up on her doorstep one day. Her friend's name was Vivian.

For her first fourteen years, Vivian had enjoyed a very good life. She lived in a quiet neighborhood in a nice house with her mother and two sisters. Then she discovered she was pregnant and at fifteen she became a teen mom. She loved little Jamar. Although his presence added meaning and joy to her life, it was definitely accompanied by its share of difficulties.

That same year Vivian's mom lost her job as a phlebotomy instructor in a large hospital. Vivian had suspected that she might be abusing the pain medication prescribed following a car accident, but now she realized that her momma had become addicted. She was melting the drugs and injecting them into her veins on a regular basis.

There was no longer any money to pay the rent or buy groceries. Soon there was not much left in the fridge except some curdled milk and a carton of moldy potato salad. When an eviction notice arrived, Vivian packed up her one-year-old baby, helped her little sister get her things together, and piled everything she could into the car. Her mom drove them to the closest hotel.

"Home" became an unsafe series of seedy motel rooms that included an unsavory string of shady people. Men became a means for her mom to pay for the room and maintain her habit. There were times Vivian's mother left to "get more money" and didn't return for days.

When things became utterly desperate, Vivian started working at a McDonald's restaurant within walking distance of her newest "home." She bought and scavenged enough food for herself and her son and her sister to live on. She used her own money to pay for the room, trying desperately to buy a little stability. But when she ran out of money, the motel manager knocked on the door and demanded immediate payment. Vivian told him he would have to talk to her mother when she returned from work, knowing full well that her mother was strung out on drugs in the bathroom tub.

A few days later, with her mother absent once again, Vivian and her son and little sister were forcibly evicted. As they stood on the side of the street waiting for someone to pick them up, Vivian realized that she couldn't keep living like this. Her friend Anna had moved to a town nearby, and she decided to join her.

Her sister didn't want to accompany her, so Vivian found her a ride to an "aunt's" house. Then she borrowed some money and made her way to the Greyhound bus station. She purchased a ticket and boarded the bus with her baby, not having a clue what to expect when they arrived at their destination.

Somehow she made her way to Anna's house. Anna's family wasn't thrilled to welcome two more needy people into their home, but they agreed to help for a few days until Vivian could find somewhere else to live.

It was Wednesday when Vivian arrived, and Anna had no intentions of missing the Teen MOPS meeting that evening. She invited Vivian to join her. If it meant free food and free diapers, Vivian knew she could sit through an hour of Bible study. So, gratefully she tagged along carrying little Jamar.

During the program that evening, each of the girls was handed a twenty-dollar bill. They were instructed to give it to someone else who really needed it. It was a tangible way for them to show gratefulness for God's blessings in their lives by passing something on to others.

Vivian could not believe that she was holding a twenty-dollar bill. Then one of the leaders handed her another twenty and whispered, "I want you to keep yours and take this one as well. I know you really need it." Tears filled Vivian's eyes. Already she knew that she had found a place where she could feel safe and loved.

Vivian and Jamar bounced from house to house, not staying at any one place for more than a few nights. But somehow Vivian managed to keep attending Teen MOPS. It was more than free food and baby items and twenty-dollar bills that kept her coming. It was a sense of knowing that this was a place where people really cared about her.

A few weeks later Teen MOPS leader, Alice, received a desperate phone call from Vivian. She and eighteen-month-old Jamar had nowhere to sleep that night, and she was afraid to stay at the city shelter. Alice told her that she would call around and try to find a safe place for her, but if she couldn't find a home, she would have to call DCF (Florida's Department of Children and Families). She explained that she couldn't allow one of "her girls" to sleep out on the streets.

Alice immediately called Barbara, a new mentor at Teen MOPS who had been assigned to Vivian's table, and asked her to pray about the situation. Although they had only met a few weeks before, Barbara felt a compelling affinity to the young teen mom and her baby. She shared the urgent prayer request with her husband and explained the dire circumstances that had brought Vivian to their town.

Nathan looked straight into Barbara's eyes and asked, "So what do you want to do about the situation?" Her eyes filled with tears and she replied, "I want to go get her." That evening Vivian and Jamar moved their few belongings into what had been Barbara and Nathan's storeroom.

Barbara naively thought that it would take only a few days and a few phone calls to find Vivian a program that would be able to help her long-term. She had no idea what difficulties she would encounter. There were three facts that made the task almost impossible:

1. Vivian was only sixteen.
2. She had a baby.
3. She was not a client of the DCF program.

There were places for girls who were sixteen to find housing, and several places that would take girls over eighteen with their babies. But there was no place for a sixteen-year-old with a child. If Vivian became a ward of DCF and was placed in a foster home, there was very little chance that she would be allowed to stay in the same home as her baby. It was even possible that she would never see him again, so that didn't appear to be an acceptable solution.

A couple of days of searching turned into a couple of weeks, which turned into a couple of months. Barbara spent a lot of time making phone calls and praying. One day, feeling rather desperate, she shared the story with Annette, her hairdresser, wondering if she might know of anyone who would be interesting in adopting Jamar. Her prayer was that a family would not only fall in love with Jamar, but would open their hearts to Vivian as well so they would not have to be separated. She knew that Jamar was all the Vivian had and that she desperately loved him.

Both Barbara and Nathan agreed that it was not possible for Vivian to stay with them once summer arrived. Both of them worked full-time jobs and their fourteen-year-old son would be home much of the time. It was not appropriate for him to be left alone with Vivian despite the trust they had in both of them. All it would take was one false accusation or rumor and their lives could be damaged forever.

Although she understood the reasoning behind the decision, Vivian was hurt. She couldn't help feeling rejected. She was being kicked out of a home once again. She began to shut down. She packed her things and decided to move in with a relative of Jamar's father whom she had recently run into. It was not a safe situation. Drug use was apparent. Barbara was distraught. She stayed in contact with Vivian and Jamar as much as possible.

A few weeks later, Barbara received a phone call from a lady named Karen. Her sister was a client of Annette's, and while having her hair trimmed she had heard about the need for a home and had called Karen. Although Karen and her husband already had four daughters of their own, they had often talked about adopting another child—preferably a little boy from another country. But Vivian's story tugged at Karen's heart. She shared the details with her husband, Ed, and they decided to see if this might be a part of God's plan for their family. Maybe they could adopt Jamar. After all, hadn't they been hoping for a little boy?

That weekend Vivian agreed to meet Karen at her home, but she expressed great concern about losing the baby she had fought so hard to protect and provide for. Without hesitation, Karen and Ed offered to open their home to both Vivian and Jamar. They promised that they would do everything they could to help Vivian stay with her son. Vivian's eyes filled with tears. "You're the only ones I've talked to who considered letting me keep him," she quietly stated.

Everyone's optimism was short lived. As soon as Vivian began to pack up her few things, the family she was living with expressed adamant opposition. They warned her not to trust Karen. They were sure this new family would find a way to separate Vivian from her son. They insisted that she stay with them. So she did.

But the living conditions she was in rapidly deteriorated. DCF became involved and soon there were rumors of them taking her baby. Vivian called Karen and begged her to take Jamar for a little while. Karen tried to talk Vivian into leaving too, but Vivian insisted that she was okay. She explained that she was getting a job and would soon have her own apartment and be able to properly care for Jamar.

She did get a job, and she did move into an apartment. When Karen dropped Jamar off to live with his mother, she peered inside. It was a nice, neat little place, but there were many unanswered questions: *How could a sixteen-year-old get an apartment? Who signed the lease?* She shared her concerns with Barbara.

Vivian obviously needed childcare while she was at work, and Karen saw this as an opportunity to stay involved in Vivian's life. She offered to help, and Vivian took her up on it.

Every morning Karen picked them up. She dropped Vivian at work and cared for Jamar the rest of the day. Each evening she drove them back to the little apartment. One evening, as she helped Vivian carry things inside, she discovered that a man was living there. *Obviously it must be his name that is on the lease* Karen reasoned. She realized that Vivian was providing for her son in the best way she knew—she had moved in with this man in exchange for a place to live.

Meanwhile, Vivian continued to attend Teen MOPS whenever she could. One night, she privately asked one of the leaders for a free pregnancy test. These tests are one of the "extras" the Teen MOPS program provides with several strings attached including pre-natal visits and ultrasounds at the clinic if the results are positive.

And this time . . . they were!

When Karen picked Vivian up the next morning, she noticed that the teenager's eyes were puffy. She had obviously been crying. "What's wrong?" Karen wanted to know. "I'm pregnant!" Vivian blurted out. Then, through her tears she looked at Karen and begged, "Will you adopt my new baby? I know I don't want to abort it, but I can't do this anymore!"

It didn't take long for Karen and her husband to agree—*this* must be the baby God had planned for them!

But God had much bigger plans than they imagined. Within a few months, not only would Karen and Ed be raising a newborn baby boy of their own, they would be adopting a teenage daughter (Vivian) while allowing her to maintain custody of her two-year-old son and raise him in their home! It was a solution and a scenario that had never crossed their minds. No one had realized that Vivian was still eligible for adoption!

God worked all the details out in an amazing way. Because DCF had become involved in Vivian's life, her adoption took place through their agency. This gave Vivian access to free medical care and a college education. Currently she is taking courses to prepare for her GED exam and she plans to enter college very soon.

Vivian has been given a new life in more than one way. While continuing to attend Teen MOPS, she accepted Jesus as her Savior. Her life is now filled with joy! She has added an energetic spark to her new family and blessed their lives in countless ways. She has taught all of them to appreciate the things they used to take for granted. Growing up, she never had the opportunity to eat with a family, so she loves dinnertime. She eagerly accompanies Karen to the grocery store and can't wait for the next time they grill out. She enjoys paging through family picture albums and discovering the history of her new family—and she is adding pages of her own.

Before joining her new family, Vivian didn't have any idea what God wanted her to look for in a husband and father for her children. Now she insists that the next man in her life will have the same priorities as her new father. She prays for a husband who will know the Lord, respect her, and be willing to work hard despite the circumstances. She prays that her son will grow to be a man of character, just like the godly man who is now his role model.

It is amazing how many lives can be touched when hope is shared. Mercedes found hope. With it she touched Anna's life. Anna passed it on to Vivian. Vivian now shares it with everyone she meets. More and more lives are transformed as hope continues its contagious journey.

A letter read at a Sunday morning service:

September 2011

Dear Church,

We are in need of some help with our Teen MOPS group. Our group has grown so much in the past year. Last November we had nine girls and were excited about that because the previous year we had only six with an average attendance of three. Now we have forty-two with thirty in regular attendance! God is definitely doing more than we can ever ask or imagine! We have had ten baptisms this past year. . .

We need help in many ways. We have plenty of clothes, but our BIGGEST need is diapers, wipes, shampoo, baby wash, lotion etc. . .

We also need help with transportation . . . not only do we have more girls now, we have had nine babies and four more due this year alone. So that makes thirteen extra seats. . . God is building this ministry and we are confident He will provide the people to help transport the girls and their babies.

We try to provide a home cooked meal for these girls as often as possible and are grateful to our Divine by Design class that provides wonderful meals every other week. This has helped tremendously because it had gotten to be more than the three of us could handle every week. If anyone would like to help with food on those other weeks, please let us know. It would be greatly appreciated.

Thanks so much,

Alice M.
Ephesians 3:20-21

Chapter 8

IS IT POSSIBLE . . .
That an Entire Church Would Join
in the Process?

As girls' lives were touched, the word about the Teen MOPS program began to spread and the numbers continued to grow—from thirty regular attendees to almost sixty. As the numbers grew, so did the need for even more transportation, mentors, food, donations, and storage space. And God faithfully provided the people and products and services necessary to meet every need.

Although the focus of the Teen MOPS program continued to be the Wednesday evening meetings that took place in a small classroom in the middle of a long hallway, this did not prove to be the time nor the place where many girls chose to give their lives to Christ. One of the goals of the leaders was to help the girls become comfortable in a larger church setting. Every week they encouraged them to attend the worship services. They offered transportation and arranged to sit with them in the sanctuary. It was there that many young moms experienced the love and affirmation of an entire congregation. It was then that they were willing to accept Christianity as a real alternative to the lives they had known.

One by one they made their way to the altar in the front of the church. One by one they knelt and asked Jesus to come into their heart and change their life. One by one they chose to signify the importance of this decision by being baptized.

Chatter around the church began to include snippets about the many new girls who were not only attending Teen MOPS, but were now showing up regularly for church services.

"Did you hear that five girls were baptized last week? They are all part of the Teen MOPS program."

"Have you seen all the cute babies in the nursery?"

The girls were astounded at the wonderful care their children received and the warm reactions they continuously experienced. People began to stop them in the hallways and take the time to coo and play with their babies. They wanted to know how old the babies were, how the mothers were doing, and if they could use any help. They really seemed to care.

The girls eagerly became members of a body of believers that accepted and loved them despite the fact that they had birthed a baby out of wedlock. They dedicated themselves to raising their children to know and serve the God whose love had rescued them. Faithfully, they found ways to bring their children to programs that were offered for them. They even began to sign up to care for other children in the church nursery and to help with other church programs.

Word of the program was spreading, not only outside on the streets, but inside the church as well. As people in the church began to notice girls' lives being transformed, they were excited to become more involved in the program. Several Sunday school classes adopted Teen MOPS as an important missional project. Bible study groups began to pray for the girls and offer assistance. Announcements about the program were made from the platform of the sanctuary.

Recently Alice made an appointment to speak with an administrator about finances. The five hundred dollars that had been budgeted annually was barely enough to purchase the new Bibles they gave each girl. She wondered if they could have more funding to help with food as well. When they checked the account, instead of finding it empty, Alice was shocked to discover that it contained two thousand dollars. The finance director had decided to double the budget and someone in the congregation had earmarked a large donation for Teen MOPS. Alice's heart and eyes overflowed with gratitude for what God was doing, not only in the lives of the girls she served, but in the lives of so many church members as well.

When it was necessary to find a larger room, one with a sink, a refrigerator, and a bathroom was made available.

A large closet was soon fitted with portable shelves and stacked with bins for use by the MOPS Shop.

Alice and Debbie shared stories about what God was doing in the lives of the Teen MOPS girls in various classes and groups that met at the church. Although they didn't actively recruit new leaders and helpers, God began to tug at many hearts. Several new people offered to transport girls to and from the meetings. They figured that since they were making the trip to church anyway, they could easily pick up a girl and her baby on the way. The conversations that took place during those car rides became an important part of the Teen MOPS experience. Many of the drivers found themselves offering to help pick up "their girls" for clinic appointments and doctor's visits. Lives became connected. Families began to pray for the girls who were becoming their friends.

When asked if they would consider using a bus for their transportation needs, Alice and Debbie shook their heads, "No, that would take away a wonderful opportunity to impact the girls' lives in a way that is impossible in a large noisy room or on a large noisy bus," Debbie replied. Alice added, "Some of the ladies are actually trading in their smaller cars for bigger ones so they can pick up more girls."

As more drivers participated, more girls were able to attend and numbers continued to increase. One of the pastors' wives became so excited about the ministry that she asked her Sunday school class to consider providing meals for the Wednesday evening meetings. Now, once a month, they drop off enough food for all the girls.

Another class decided to throw a Baby Shower once a year—complete with decorations, games and presents. Any girl who has a baby that calendar year is honored. At their first party, eighteen girls were showered with gifts and love.

Other classes now donate diapers and baby wipes on a regular basis and stay in close contact in case other needs arise. At one meeting, a teenager mentioned that she would really like to use her "Mommy Bucks" to purchase a baby swing. However, there wasn't one available. This need was announced, and when the young mom arrived the next week, there was a swing waiting for her. As soon as she saw it, she burst into tears. "This is exactly the same one I saw in the store and I prayed that I could have for my baby!" She laughed and cried at the same time.

Church members began to hand out fliers at doctors' offices and post them in stores. One noticeably pregnant teenager was handed one as she waited at a bus stop. The next week, she called the number on the flier to ask for a ride to the meeting.

Individuals began offering services such as free haircuts and gift cards for products in local stores. A young lady crochets one-of-a-kind hats for each of the new babies. Several men provide venison from their hunting trips each fall. A large men's group that meets on Wednesday evenings carries their leftover food down the hall and packages it up for the girls to take home. Most significantly, many church members are now investing time in prayer.

There is no doubt that many teenage girls' lives are being changed by the efforts and outpouring of love from the members at First Baptist Church at the Mall in Lakeland, Florida. But something else is evident as well: many church members' lives have been transformed by the relationships they now have with the teenagers God asked them to serve.

Pastor Jay Dennis[20] described the impact of the Teen MOPS program this way, "Teen MOPS is the most significant ministry we have in our church. Not only does it affect the eternal destiny of so many girls, but it has changed the atmosphere of our church. As we have gotten to know the girls involved, it has brought us joy, broadened our horizons, and given us a new perspective on teen motherhood." He added, "We started by reaching out to them, but now they are the ones reaching out to us."

Chapter 9
_____

IS IT POSSIBLE . . .
For the Surrounding Community to
Embrace the Difference?

Not only have the lives of teenage girls and their babies been affected by the Teen MOPS program in Lakeland, Florida, so have the lives of all those who assist with the program in any way. And the benefits of the program are now reaching far beyond the walls of the church that hosts them. Changes are becoming apparent in the surrounding community as well.

When Alice first stepped in as a leader in the Teen MOPS program, she realized that there were many more young ladies in the community who needed to experience the love and acceptance the program had to offer. That's when she first designed a flier and made it available to other agencies in town that work with teen moms. The reaction was anything but warm. As one of the fliers was shoved back at her, she was told, "These girls have enough going on in their lives. They don't need to add God to the mix!" However, after noticing significant changes in the lives of girls who attend Teen MOPS, that same program called Alice back and asked for fliers.

Other agencies did the same. High school counselors began to keep flyers on their desks. Programs struggling to rehabilitate teen girls who were in trouble with the law began to partner with Teen MOPS. When fourteen-year-old Sharonda was caught shoplifting with a group of friends, she was convicted and sentenced to probation, which included fifteen hours of community service. Her probation officer noticed that she was about eight months pregnant, so he tried to find a simple, yet meaningful, solution. He asked Sharonda if she was involved in any community organizations. She told him that she had attended Teen MOPS a couple of times.

The officer checked out the program and was impressed by what it offered. He then called Teen MOPS leader Alice and asked if she would be willing to sign off on Sharonda's hours to fulfill probation requirements. Alice quickly agreed. She had been praying for a way to keep the indifferent young lady involved.

Sharonda fulfilled her court obligation, and a year later she is still attending Teen MOPS. She thanks God for the wisdom of the probation officer who forever changed the direction of her life and the future of her child. Since then several other girls have completed court assignments and grown to appreciate the encouragement they received and the opportunities they were offered through Teen MOPS.

Guest speakers from Florida's Department of Children and Families have been invited to speak to the girls, as have volunteers who work with the Guardian ad litem program, and personnel from the Sheriff's department. The leaders realize how important it is for these young moms to comprehend that such agencies exist to help them, not to apprehend or demoralize them.

It has been discovered that partnership with local agencies can make a significant difference when lives are in danger. And the positive results can be multiplied when the assistance is reciprocated. When it was discovered that Julie, one of the girls attending Teen MOPS, was the victim of extreme domestic abuse, the help of a residential facility was enlisted. Although the program does not allow residents to communicate with anyone outside the facility, it does allow them to receive incoming mail. So the Teen MOPS leaders initiated a prayer and letter-writing campaign for the young lady they had referred. It was such a success that they decided to reach out to other young women at the facility. Prayer partners (including girls in the Teen MOPS program) now write letters and pray on a regular basis for several of the young women involved in the program.

Julie will complete her residential training very soon and will have her GED. She has already been reunited with her baby and is caring for her in the facility. She will begin a new life completely separate from the abusive lifestyle that was once her norm. She will have prayer partners from Teen MOPS who are eager to partner with her in life as well.

Often the girls' backgrounds require more intricate and extensive guidance than the leaders in Teen MOPS are able to provide. For this reason, they recently partnered with a counseling agency that will meet with the girls individually and help them work through issues that could otherwise sabotage their futures. This arrangement provides a level of security for leaders who are not always equipped to deal with the complicated issues associated with their pasts.

Guest speakers from local businesses such as Chick-fil-A have offered to train the girls how to apply for a job, how to fill out a resume, and how to dress, act, and answer questions during a job interview. When they discover that the manager of a company is willing to sit down and talk with them, the girls' confidence is greatly increased. When they realize that the unfamiliar world that exists outside of their own tiny cosmos is not seeking to destroy them, they begin to have hope. It is evident in their eyes.

Several charitable organizations have begun to offer items that they know will benefit the girls. Compassion House, a local facility, packs special food boxes for girls who otherwise could not adequately provide for their children. When baby items such as high chairs or strollers are donated, they notify Teen MOPS in case there is a specific need. The local Florida Baptist Children's Home supplies diapers and formula, as does a local pregnancy center.

Based on the success of the Teen MOPS program, as well as the desires of the girls whose lives are being changed, a ministry called *Man Up* opened its doors last month. They are now reaching out to teen fathers with the message of God's love. Their goal is to help them biblically fulfill their role in the lives of their offspring.

To more significantly impact the lives of their children, an effort is being made to reach out to other family members of the teen moms as well. Mercedes (whose story is told in chapter 6) was concerned that her brother Robert was getting involved with the wrong group of guys. One Sunday when Debbie and Blake picked her up for church, she asked them to pray for him.

Blake intentionally began to develop a relationship with Robert. Knowing that he needed a ride to a job interview, Blake offered to pick him up. He gave him tips along the way. He waited for Robert to finish the interview and then took him to lunch. On the way home, he invited Robert to come to church with them since they were already picking up Mercedes and Jamar. To everyone's surprise, the next Sunday, he was dressed and ready.

All it took was a little interest and involvement in his life for Robert to realize that he, too, wanted what his sister had—a relationship with Jesus Christ. Not many weeks later, he was baptized and Blake presented him with a brand new Bible—his very own; his very first. It even had his name engraved on the cover. That Sunday afternoon Robert showed up at the house and asked Blake if he would teach him how to use it. They spent the rest of the day studying the Bible together.

Every week, Robert now carries that Bible with him to church and Sunday school, trying his best to find each passage that is being studied. Because his father was in and out of jail most of his life, he never had a good role model to pattern his life after. "Mr. Blake" is now the example of the man Robert hopes to become.

What was meant to be a small gathering specifically designed to meet the needs of a few teenage moms, is now impacting lives all over the community. It is evident that God is working in a powerful way.

Chapter 10
—————

IS IT POSSIBLE . . .
To Change the Statistics?

As you have read the stories in this book, you may have found yourself thinking: *I'm happy that someone has stepped in to help these struggling teenage moms, but I'm not really sure that this is how we should handle the problem. Shouldn't we be focusing more of our efforts on preventing teen pregnancies rather than caring for the girls after they conceive?*

Great point! And this is precisely the path my thoughts traveled when I was first approached about writing this book. However, I have learned a lot over the past several months, and what I have learned has completely changed my mind. I have researched the generational cycles of teen pregnancy; I have investigated the underlying causes; I have studied the overwhelming statistics; but mostly, I have loved and lived alongside some of the girls.

In the process, I have discovered that, despite all the efforts to promote prevention, either through abstinence education or easier access to contraception, nothing has proven to work. Expansive studies (like those of Levine, 2012)[21] convincingly confirm that there is no silver bullet that will solve this particular social and moral issue.

Notice, I did not categorize out-of-wedlock teen pregnancy merely as a moral issue, because it is much more than that. The legacy of teen motherhood that is so often passed down from one generation to another is very much a social matter as well. In some families, it has almost become an unwelcomed expectation. One of the girls who attends Teen MOPS explained that she became pregnant because her mother had encouraged—almost insisted—that she have sex with her boyfriend. "You gotta give it up or you'll lose him," was her parenting advice.

Addressing teen childbearing requires tackling the social, and often economic, problems that surround it. Most of the girls attending Teen MOPS come from unstable homes. Many have alcohol- or drug-addicted parents. Some are homeless, and almost all have been abused. One girl interviewed for this book was born while her mother was in prison. Another was sold when she was a year old for drug money, a fact of which she is fully aware. Few of these girls have any framework that will support our well-intentioned teachings on prevention.

But others, like Mallory, whose story is told in Chapter 1, were raised in loving, functioning homes. Their pregnancy was not a part of a generational legacy, nor was it a matter of social conditioning. It was simply a matter of emotions and expediency—two factors that greatly influence a majority of teenage decisions despite impassioned education to the contrary.

Preventative education having failed, once a teenage girl becomes pregnant she suddenly finds herself ensnared by the alarming statistics and negative expectations we explored in Chapter 2. We looked at the probabilities of substandard education, financial difficulty, and relationship dilemmas that face a teen mother.

- But this is where programs such as Teen MOPS can intervene and make a difference!
- This is when girls are willing to listen and learn!
- This is how lives and legacies can be transformed to prevent future pregnancies and discontinue generational patterns!
- This is why we need more programs that are willing to risk ridicule to reap rewards!

We can and must take the challenge. We must stop looking at teen moms as girls who have "laid in their bed and now have to make it." As one Teen MOPS leader put it, "The only difference between teen moms and everyone else is that they have to carry the evidence of their sin everywhere they go."

We really can help them defy the statistics and change our society's expectations. We really can break the cycle and transform the legacies they pass on to their children. Here are just a few examples of expectations that can and must be shattered:

1. You will never graduate from high school.

Sophie couldn't wait for Christmas day to give her Dad his present. The year 2012 had not been easy. Eight months earlier she sat down across the table from him and shared the fact that she was pregnant. Tears welled up in his eyes and all he managed to say was, "Promise me you will graduate from high school. Tell me you will get a diploma." She nodded as tears filled her eyes as well. But she had no idea if she could really fulfill such a promise.

Then one day she heard about the brand new *Man Up* program for teen fathers. It was something she wanted her boyfriend to be involved in, because she had heard that it might help keep him connected to her and their child. So she bargained with him that if he attended *Man Up*, she would attend Teen MOPS. She came and enjoyed the program. It gave her the tools and the courage to continue her education. It gave her new friendships she could count on for support.

Many times over the next few months, Sophie's father looked at his daughter apprehensively and reminded her, "Remember, you promised me you'd get your diploma."

She had not forgotten—not for one minute. And she did it! She graduated in December. She couldn't wait for Christmas day to see him unwrap the gift she had promised him. But excitement got the best of her, and she slipped her diploma into his hands a few days early. When he realized what he was holding, he was too overwhelmed to speak. Tears rolled down his cheeks as he hugged her. The baby was due in a few weeks, but he knew everything would be okay. Sophie credits the Teen MOPS leaders with providing the encouragement that kept her on track to fulfill her father's dreams. She realizes that they will be there for her as she raises her baby to know and love the Lord.

And then there's Trina. Trina loved Teen MOPS. She attended not only on Wednesday evenings, but she began to attend worship services in the big, beautiful sanctuary as well. Soon she gave her life to Christ.

Then, in July 2012, her mother suddenly lapsed into a diabetic coma and never recovered. Together, Trina and her dad made it through the funeral, but it wasn't long before she began to make unwise decisions that were changing the direction of her life. Knowing he needed to help his daughter before she messed up her life completely, Trina's father made a deal with her. He itemized a list and told her that if she stopped doing the negative things he had listed, he would stop smoking and drinking and he would go to church with her.

She took him up on it. Together they walked into the big sanctuary and found a place to sit near some of the other teen moms. Together they sang and listened and prayed. Together they returned the next week. It was only a few more weeks until her father walked to the altar and gave his life to Jesus Christ.

Trina's life is back on course and she will graduate in May. Her father will be there cheering as she walks across the stage to receive her diploma.

Many other girls have graduated because of the support they have received from the program. Five young ladies walked across the stage at First Baptist Church at the Mall with the rest of the graduates being honored last May. One of them was in the National Honor Society. And the truth is, when you educate a mom you educate a whole family.

2. There go your dreams of college.

Not all of the girls who graduate from high school while attending Teen MOPS will go on to college. But, although the program is young, some already have. Caryssa is just one example. After delivering her baby and graduating from high school, she became a paramedic. She loved her work so much that she decided to continue her education. She is currently back in school and will graduate soon as a Registered Nurse.

3. You will always be financially dependent.

As I mentioned before, once a year, each of the girls at Teen MOPS is given a twenty-dollar bill to pass on to someone who is in greater need than they are. At the next meeting they report how they chose to deliver this blessing and how God used it. This training tool allows them to experience the joy of sharing with others, rather than always being on the receiving end.

Last month, one of the girls handed her twenty-dollar bill to a man who was checking out in front of her at the grocery store. He only had enough change for one can of soup. So she handed him the extra money, and he immediately purchased more groceries. She is hoping to be able to help him more in the future.

Another teen mom helped an elderly lady remove a stray cat from her house. As they were looking for the cat she discovered that the lady didn't have any food in her cupboards and the refrigerator was empty. Her twenty dollars combined with a few dollars she borrowed from her mom were enough to buy groceries to last a few days. (She did eventually catch the cat and remove it from the lady's house.)

Another girl gave her money to a man who roams the neighborhood collecting cans so he can earn enough money to buy food. "I felt warm and full inside when I did," she told the group.

Someone else helped a lady at the pharmacy who otherwise couldn't have afforded her prescription.

The stories go on and on as the girls learn the joy of giving and continue to do so throughout the year. They are beginning to understand how much better it is to give than to receive.

4. You will never be able to sustain a healthy relationship.

Before attending Teen MOPS, Phyllis felt like an outcast. She felt like her parents, who had been pillars in their church, were completely ashamed of her. They hated the boy who was their grandbaby's father. They made it difficult for her to see him. Her younger brother and sister felt that she had betrayed them.

Phyllis no longer felt welcome at the youth group she had been such an active part of. She wasn't sure how her life could possibly result in anything positive. Then she began to attend Teen MOPS. There she felt free to be honest and open about what was going on in her life. She found a place where she could evaluate her own feelings and begin to understand those of her family members. She was able to embrace becoming a mom and set about to make something out of the life she thought she had ruined.

Not only did she graduate from high school, she completed culinary school and became a pastry chef. But, most importantly, while attending Teen MOPS she restored her relationship with Christ. And, in the process, He helped restore her relationships with her parents and her baby's father.

A year after their baby girl was born, Phyllis and Jonathan were married, and after two years of marriage she continues to boast about their happy relationship. At twenty-two years old, she still faithfully attends Teen MOPS, except now she is a mentor! She is passing on the encouragement as well as the admonishment she received.

She knows the girls need it. She softly reprimands the girls who become discouraged and want to give up. "If I can work and go to school and raise a baby, and have a happy marriage, so can you! I don't want to see you give up. You've got to trust God and go for it. He has a plan, but you have to trust Him and work hard. He will make everything work out."

Not only are these teen moms defying the statistics in their own lives, they are impacting other lives in their community as well. When a mother called Teen MOPS leader Alice to ask if she and her teenage daughter could visit the program, Alice asked if the girl was pregnant or if she had already had her baby.

"Neither," the mother replied. "She thinks she wants to get pregnant, and I thought that maybe if she could talk to teens who were already in that situation, she might find out that this is not really what she wants." Alice saw this as an opportunity for the girls to help someone else make a better choice than they had, so she invited the girl and her mother to attend.

They decided to come twice to observe and interact. After watching the teen play with the babies and laugh with their mothers during her first visit, the Teen MOPS leadership grimaced. "Oh no," they thought, "she is really going to want to have her own baby now."

However, as the girls began to interact with their guest during her second visit, they started explaining how rough it is to be a teen mom. One by one they shared their stories. They told about their struggles keeping up in school, babies not sleeping, doctor visits, etc. They explained that they had no time for themselves and absolutely no time to spend with any of their friends. They described how difficult life was compared to before they became pregnant.

Finally Alice asked, "How many of you girls, if *your* mother had been wise enough to let you see what it was *really* like, would have chosen *not* to get pregnant?" Seventy-five percent of the girls raised their hands. The visiting teenager's eyes grew large as she listened and observed. She realized that, although these girls loved their babies, they were physically and emotionally exhausted from a role they were unprepared to assume.

Later the Teen MOPS leaders heard back from the mom, who thanked them for their "intervention." Her daughter no longer wanted to become pregnant. She decided to wait until she is much older and her life is much more prepared.

Society says these girls are too broken to accomplish anything worthwhile. But broken people are the very people God used all through His scriptures to change the world. According to the first chapter of Matthew's gospel, three broken women factor significantly into the genealogy of Jesus Christ. There is Tamar (verse 3) who slept with her own father-in-law, Rahab (verse 5) who was a well-known prostitute, and Bathsheba (verse 6) who was married to Uriah when she slept with King David. Even Mary,

Jesus' own mother, was probably a teen mom, and she was definitely considered broken by others in her society.

As teen moms begin to accept their significance in God's eyes, they begin to understand their potential. They begin to accept His boundaries for their lives. They become brave enough to say, "If sex is the only way I can keep a man in my life then I don't want him." They learn what love really is. *And they teach what they learn to their children!*

This is one concrete way that real societal change can take place. This is one actual way that statistics can be altered. This is one tangible way that we can prevent recurring teen pregnancies and break the generational cycle. Sometimes it requires brokenness before beauty can be revealed. We have to remember that teen moms are not just promiscuous girls with great big problems. They are little girls who need a great big Savior.

If more Christians and churches became involved in helping them, think how many more lives and statistics could be changed!

FAMILY TREE
By Matthew West
From the album "The Story of Your Life."

(This song has become a source of hope for many of the young moms who attend Teen MOPS.)

You didn't ask for this. Nobody ever would.
Caught in the middle of this dysfunction.
It's your sad reality. It's your messed up family tree.
And you're left with all these questions.

Are you gonna be like your father (or mother) was?
And his father (or her mother) was?
Do you have to carry what they've handed down?

No, this is not your legacy! This is not your destiny!
Yesterday does not define you.
No, this is not your legacy! This is not your meant to be!
I can break the chains that bind you.

I have a dream for you. It's better than where you've been.
It's bigger than your imagination.
You're gonna find real love. And you're gonna hold your kids.
You'll change the course of generations.

No, this is not your legacy! This is not your destiny!
Yesterday does not define you.
No, this is not your legacy! This is not your meant to be!
I can break the chains that bind you.

Cause you're my child. You're my chosen.
You are loved. You are loved.

And I will restore all that was broken.
You are loved. You are loved.

And just like the seasons change—winter into spring,
You're bringing new life to your family tree now.
Yes you are. You are. Oh, Oh, Ooh.

No, this will be your legacy. This will be your destiny.
Yesterday did not define you.
No, this will be your legacy. This will be your meant to be.
I can break the chains that bind you.

Chapter 11

IS IT POSSIBLE . . .
That God Wants You to
Become Involved?

This book was not written as an endorsement for the Teen MOPS program—as significant as this program is. It is not meant to bring glory to First Baptist Church at the Mall—as commendable as their ministry in the Lakeland community has been. It was not penned in order to applaud the women who offered their lives and allowed their experiences to change the legacies of so many teen moms—as worthy as they are. It isn't even an attempt to chronicle the stories of the young moms whose lives have been so drastically transformed—as amazing as they are turning out to be.

No, this book was written to challenge you. It is a request for you to focus your heart in a way that allows you to see more than just the shadows of the teenage moms who have been shoved to the perimeter of our society. I'm asking you to get close enough to look into their eyes and see what God sees. I'm encouraging you to reach out your arms and invite these little children to "come unto you" just as Jesus always did.

The very fact that you are still reading indicates that God has placed a sensitivity in your heart to the issues teen moms face. You may even feel a connection somewhere in your soul. But, more than likely, you are wrestling with some form of resistance in your mind: *it's just so complicated; so time consuming; so far outside of my comfort zone.*

Let me ask you a question: *Was anything Jesus ever called his disciples to do simple?* I can't think of a single task that didn't stretch far beyond their ability to reason or perform:

- You want us to leave our families and our jobs to follow you and you can't even tell us where we will sleep at night? Seriously?
- How on earth are we supposed to feed all those people seated on this desolate, rural hillside? There's no McDonald's anywhere in sight!
- You honestly expect us to stay calm when our boat is about to capsize in the middle of a hurricane?
- If I say I know you, I will be crucified! What happened to the part about you becoming a King and me sitting on a throne next to you? This isn't anything like what I thought I signed up for!

Working with teenagers is never easy—especially when they are tangled in the traumas of pregnancies and parenting! But I can promise you that if Jesus is calling you to such a ministry, it will be rewarding! More rewarding than you can ever imagine!

As you know from Alice's story (Chapter 3), all it takes is one willing heart to begin a chain of events that will impact an entire community. If you are willing to trust Him, God will take care of all the details. He will equip you in every way necessary. He will soften calloused hearts, fill empty spaces, provide necessary tools, and continually demonstrate His power. Look at some of the blessings He promises in Isaiah 58 to those who serve the needy:

- This is the kind of fasting I want: Free those who are wrongly imprisoned; lighten the burden of those who work for you. Let the oppressed go free, and remove the chains that bind people.
- Share your food with the hungry, and give shelter to the homeless. Give clothes to those who need them, and do not hide from relatives who need your help.

  Then your salvation will come like the dawn, and your wounds will quickly heal. Your godliness will lead you forward, and the glory of the Lord will protect you from behind.

  Then when you call, the Lord will answer. 'Yes, I am here,' he will quickly reply. "Remove the heavy yoke of oppression. Stop pointing your finger and spreading vicious rumors!

- Feed the hungry, and help those in trouble. Then your light will shine out from the darkness, and the darkness around you will be as bright as noon.

The Lord will guide you continually, giving you water when you are dry and restoring your strength. You will be like a well-watered garden, like an ever-flowing spring.

Some of you will rebuild the deserted ruins of your cities. Then you will be known as a rebuilder of walls and a restorer of homes (Isaiah 58:6-12).

Do not fall prey to the notion that somehow your life experiences exempt you from accomplishing remarkable things for God, because they do not. Do not think for one minute that you have not been called to serve Him just the way you are, because you have. I am convinced that far too many of us view the hardships in our lives as trials we must endure rather than training tools God intends for us to use.

For we are God's masterpiece. He has created us anew in Christ Jesus, so we can do the good things he planned for us long ago (Ephesians 2:10).

This book was written to encourage and motivate you regardless of how unprepared and ill-equipped you may feel. It is a challenge to step out in faith if you feel God stirring your heart in any way.

Here are some steps that might make it simpler:

1. *Start with prayer.* Then continue to prioritize prayer in every facet of this amazing journey. We cannot achieve anything significant without God's presence and power controlling the process. Prayer is our "declaration of dependence" on Him. The more we admit our weakness and inadequacy, the more freedom He has to accomplish *His* purposes.

2. When you feel God's prompting, *share your feelings with others who may be willing to walk beside you.* If you are in a church setting, don't hesitate to communicate with the staff. Share with them how God is leading you. Ask them to pray with you. From the very beginning you must make it clear that you are not interested in a patronizing program that will allow the girls to sit around and be victims. People must understand that your ultimate goal is to lead young moms into a relationship with Jesus Christ. In addition you want to encourage and empower them to be successful in our society. Encourage those you share with to pray with you about what role God may have for them. Then get ready to watch God work as doors are opened and obstacles are removed.

3. All the while, *keep your eyes open for teen moms who need God's love.* It may seem like a slow process at first, but remember, it only takes one girl like Mercedes to experience God's life-changing power and suddenly dozens more will be eager to participate.

4. *Seek support from an organization that is already reaching out to teen moms.* I know that MOPS (Mothers of Preschoolers, International) provides a supporting staff, resource materials, and training for groups who apply to become a part of their Teen MOPS program. So does Young Life through their program called Young Lives. These and other programs are ready to assist you in any way they can. Don't waste the wisdom God has already given them.

5. *Begin to network in order to take advantage of the assets that are already available in your community.* Don't be shy about asking local businessmen and women to invest their resources and time. Invite various health professionals to share at your meetings. Communicate with high school counselors. Contact local law enforcement agencies. You will be amazed at how many individuals and organizations are eager to help when you present them with an opportunity.

6. *Don't get discouraged!* Satan isn't going to want you to succeed, but remember that God is the One who is in control, and He is the One to whom you report.

7. The next time someone (like me) randomly surveys your church or organization to discover what programs and resources are available for teen moms, *share with them all the awesome things that God is doing!*

As I mentioned before, I am convinced that teen mothers and their babies are some of the "widows and orphans" of our day. They are the ones we are commanded to serve in the book of James: *Pure and genuine religion in the sight of God the Father means caring for orphans and widows in their distress . . . (James 1:27)* These young women are doomed to repeat the legacy of despair handed down from generation to generation unless we step in to offer them hope—the hope that can only be found in Jesus Christ—accompanied by the help of someone who will walk through life beside them.

I asked some of the pastors at First Baptist Church at the Mall in Lakeland, Florida, what they would like to share with someone starting a program for teen moms in their church. Senior Pastor Dr. Jay Dennis replied, "I would strongly encourage other pastors to allow a program like Teen MOPS to change their church. If the pastor and staff buy into it, then the whole church will buy in. The girls involved will feel affirmed and their lives will be changed. Any size church can get involved. The leaders in the program must be given time on the platform and space in the bulletin to share their needs and prayer requests. The whole church should be given the opportunity to embrace the program." He added, "This is a ministry that will not only change the girls' lives and their children's, it will affect your whole church. We need more churches to get involved."

Pastor Jerry Goodell[22], the Senior Associate Pastor of Pastoral Care, cautioned, "If you want everything nice and tidy and neat, this program is not going to work for you. You have to be flexible—roll with what the girls need. We can't expect them to come in and act like us, behave like us, and worship like us. We're the ones who have to be flexible."

What looks good on paper doesn't always translate into something that meets needs out in the streets. What sounds good in a planning meeting doesn't always work in an abusive home. But that's okay. Things don't always have to look clean and make sense to create change. As one of the Teen MOPS leaders put it, "This ministry is ninety-nine percent love and one percent logic."

There is one more quote that struck my heart as I embarked on the amazing privilege and process of writing this book. It will always be with me: "People ask me all the time why I want to serve in Teen MOPS. That answer is not hard. I want to be where Jesus is! I want to watch Him transform brokenness into beauty. I want to watch Him grow legacies out of the ashes! I want to see God move and breathe life and hope and strength into situations that aren't always amazing. I want to watch God take a group of people humbled and focused on His will for their lives and use them for His glory. I want to watch God match His righteousness with His compassion and break bondage! I want to be where Jesus is, for as long as

He lets me because my girls (the teen moms He allows me to serve) are amazing!" *(Meagan Goepferich, a volunteer with the Teen Mops program in Lakeland, Florida)*[23]

When we step out in faith, we must be prepared to watch God work—because He will! He wants to amaze us! Do you want to be amazed by God? The answer to the question posed throughout this book is undeniably affirmative: with God's help we can transform the lives and legacies of teenage moms!

ENDNOTES

Introduction

1. Guttmacher Institute, *U.S. Teenage Pregnancies, Births and Abortions: National and State Trends and Trends by Race and Ethnicity* (New York: Guttmacher Institute, 2010), 2.

2. ibid. 7.

3. Mississippi Law Blog, *Adoption, Mentoring and Teen Pregnancy,* (Nov. 06, 2012).

4. Dr. Lorraine V. Klerman, *Another Chance: Preventing Additional Births to Teen Mothers*, (The National Campaign to Prevent Teen Pregnancy, 2004), 1.

5. Hartford Institute for Religion Research, hirr. hartsem.edu/megachurch/database.html.

Chapter 1

6. Unless otherwise indicated, all the names in this book have been changed in order to maintain confidentiality of the teenage girls and their families.

Chapter 2

7. Stayteen.org: *The National Campaign to Prevent Teen and Unplanned Pregnancy*, (2013), accessed via www.stayteen.org.

8. crihb.org/files/statistic_on_teen_pregnancy.pdf

9. Guttmacher Institute, *U.S. Teenage Pregnancies*, (2010), 7.

10. Melissa Schettini Kearney and Phillip B. Levine, "*Why is the Teen Birth Rate in the United States So High and Why Does It Matter?*" (Working Paper 17965 for the National Bureau of Economic Research, Cambridge, MA, 2012), 1.

11. Kearney and Levine, *Teen Birth Rate*, (2012), 19-20.

12. Stayteen.org, (2013)

13. Posted by agnesrobi, *I am a Teen Mom* (The Youth Booth—Youth Services, Nov. 2010).

14. Stayteen.org, *Teen Mom 3: Pros and Cons*, (2013)

15. Stayteen.org, *The National Campaign*, (2013)

16. Saul D. Hoffman and Rebecca A. Maynard, eds, *Kids Having Kids: Economic Costs and Social Consequences of Teen Pregnancy* (Washington, DC: Urban Institute, 2008), Chapter 5.

17 Stayteen.org, (2013)

Chapter 5

18. Liz Curtis Higgs, *Bad Girls of the Bible and What We Can Learn From Them*, (Colorado Springs, CO: WaterBrook Press, 1999).

19. Jonny Diaz, *More Beautiful You: A Study in "True Beauty,"* (Tulsa, OK: Harrison House, 2010).

Chapter 8

20. This pastor's name has not been changed.

Chapter 10

21. Kearney and Levine, *Teen Birth Rate*, (2012), 2.

Chapter 11

22. This pastor's name has not been changed.
23. This volunteer's name has not been changed.

ABOUT THE AUTHOR

Gwen Diaz grew up as a missionary kid in West Africa before moving to the US and graduating from the University of Pennsylvania with a BS in nursing. There she met Ed Diaz, and together they raised four sons, all of whom are grown, married and following Jesus. With ten grandchildren, their house is often chaotic, and always filled with fun.

When she isn't writing, Gwen stays busy packing diaper bags. As founder of the charity OH MY Baby, she desires that no new mother will leave the hospital without the items necessary to nurture her baby through the first few weeks of life. Gwen is passionate about teaching God's truths to the next generation and often speaks at Bible conferences. Gwen and Ed reside in Central Florida.

Connect with Gwen:
www.gwendiazcom
E-mail: zmbj@aol.com